BREAKAWAY

BREAKAWAY

Samuel Abt

On the Road with the Tour de France

Random House New York

All rights reserved under International and Pan-American Copyright Conventions.
Published in the United States by Random House, Inc., New York, and
simultaneously in Canada by Random House of Canada Limited, Toronto.

Grateful acknowledgment is made to Random House, Inc., for permission to reprint
an excerpt from "Fleet Visit," by W.H. Auden, from *W.H. Auden: Collected Poems,*
edited by Edward Mendelson. Copyright © 1955 by W.H. Auden.

Library of Congress Cataloging in Publication Data
Abt, Samuel.
Breakaway : on the road with the Tour de France.
1. Tour de France (Bicycle race) I. Title.
GV1049.2.T68A 1985   796.6'0944   85-2025
ISBN 0-394-54679-2

Manufactured in the United States of America

9 8 7 6 5 4 3 2

First Edition

Design by Bernard Klein

This book, with love and respect, is for my children,
Claire, Phoebe, and John

The pride of lions: do not shut them up in Zoos.
The pride of your dogs: let them not grow fat. Love
the pride of your fellow-partisans, and allow them
no self-pity.

—*Karen Blixen,* Out of Africa

Acknowledgments

I owe thanks to many people who encouraged and assisted me in the work on this book. First among them is Barbara Bell, who discovered professional bicycling in our family and finally persuaded me to watch it with her. Any race day spent traveling with her is truly a breakaway.

Two other good companions are David Walsh of the Irish Press Group and John Wilcockson of the *Times of London,* with whom I followed the 1984 Tour de France. Their insights are plentifully obvious in this book, and I hope they enjoyed my company as much as I did theirs. I appreciate especially the friendship of Phil Liggett, Geoffrey Nicholson, Mike Price, and Charles Burgess among the multitude of reporters always willing to share observations and quotes. I am also pleased to acknowledge my debt to the vast staff of the newspaper *L'Equipe,* which often did the reporting no single foreigner could do. Finally, I give special thanks for their support to Joseph Vecchione, sports editor of *The New York Times,* and to my agent, Ed Victor.

BREAKAWAY

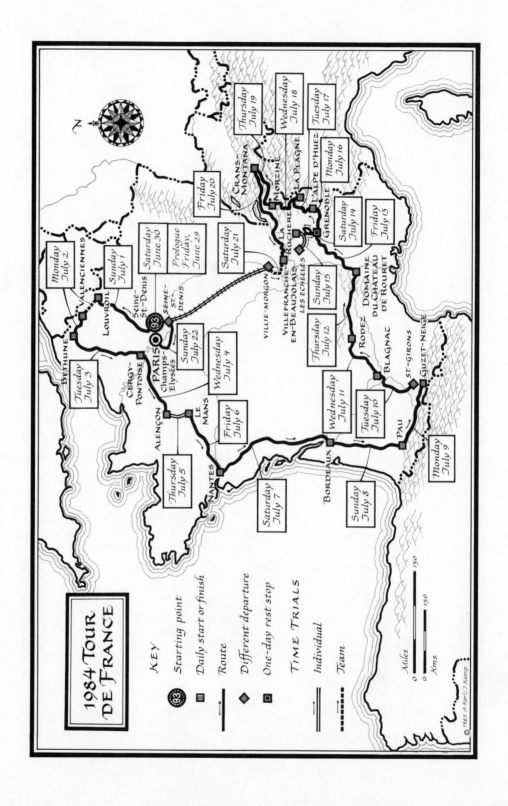

1984 TOUR DE FRANCE

KEY

- Starting point
- Daily start or finish
- Route
- Different departure
- One-day rest stop

TIME TRIALS

- Individual
- Team

N

Miles
0   150

Kms.
0   150

© 1985 A. Karl/J. Kemp

Monday July 2
Sunday July 1
Saturday June 30
Prologue Friday, June 29
Saturday July 21
Friday July 20
CRANS-MONTANA
Thursday July 19
Wednesday July 18
MORZINE
Tuesday July 17
LA PLAGNE
ALPE D'HUEZ
Monday July 16
GRENOBLE
Saturday July 14
Friday July 13
LA RUCHERE
LES ECHELLES
DOMAINE DU CHATEAU DE ROUNEL
VALENCIENNES
LOUVROIL
SEINE-ST-DENIS
Seine-St-Denis
VILLIE-MORGON
VILLEFRANCHE-EN-BEAUJOLAIS
Sunday July 15
Thursday July 12
RODEZ
BETHUNE
Tuesday July 3
CERGY-PONTOISE
PARIS
Champs-Elysées
Sunday July 22
Wednesday July 4
LE MANS
ALENÇON
Friday July 6
BLAGNAC
ST-GIRONS
GUZET-NEIGE
Wednesday July 11
Tuesday July 10
PAU
Monday July 9
NANTES
Thursday July 5
Saturday July 7
BORDEAUX
Sunday July 8

*F*ar up the road, spectators had already
*jammed the switchback curves of L'Alpe-d'Huez. The police finally
gave up trying to estimate the size of the crowd and could only say it
was many more than the usual 300,000 to 400,000 who waited each
year for the bicycle riders in the Tour de France to climb to the peak.
This Sunday morning in July, while the sun burned off traces of fog
in the valley and melted a bit of the glaciers permanently atop the
French Alps, the crowd was waiting for one rider. "Allez, Simon," the
banners said. By then it was over.*

*Far down the road, on the Chapelle-Blanche hill, precisely at kilo-
meter 95 of the day's 223-kilometer stage, Pascal Simon had ended his
race. The television motorcycle that had been hovering for a week let
millions of Frenchmen watch as Simon tried to climb the hill, grimacing with the pain of a left shoulder blade broken in a fall. He had
strength in one arm only, and his unbalanced bicycle wobbled; the
other riders stood on the pedals and put their weight forward on their
shoulders as they thrust, but Simon had to remain seated. Doctors had
been taping his shoulder blade each day and treating it with heat, ice,
and laser beams, but Simon's pain was obvious as he labored up the
hill. Sweat illuminated his face and darkened the back of his yellow
jersey, the symbol that Simon led the Tour de France. Another rider
might win an individual day's race, a stage, but there was no special
jersey for this; only the leader in overall elapsed time from start to
finish of the three-week race wore the yellow jersey. In the rainbow of
team colors, the yellow jersey was the one the crowds looked for.*

*Simon's mouth began to hang open as he gulped for breath. Then
he coasted onto the shoulder of the road and made the bicyclist's
traditional gesture of surrender: he put his feet to the ground while*

the race continued and unpinned the cloth with his number on his back. "I'm very sad and very sorry," Simon said, "but the pain is too great." He turned his bicycle over to a mechanic for his Peugeot team and climbed into an ambulance to finish the trip to L'Alpe-d'Huez.

He had been saying for a week that the pain was growing worse but that he did not want to quit while he was still wearing the yellow jersey. As he coasted out of the race, he was 11 minutes behind the day's front-runners and had lost the yellow jersey.

○

Bernard Vallet turned professional in 1976, the same year as Bernard Hinault. "One of us just took off and the other, I mean me, blew it," Vallet remembered years later. "My first year as a professional reassured me: good results in Paris-Nice, the National, and the Dauphiné Libéré. I thought I was capable of having a pretty career. The next year I had a good Tour de France, but I had to improve to be a star and the trouble was that my health was bad. By the end of the season I was exhausted. It got worse. Then came the bad year, 1978, the catastrophic year. All kinds of health problems, including hepatitis. The doctors couldn't understand it. I didn't race in the Dauphiné or in the Tour —a terrible blow, my worst memory. I even thought of quitting.

"It was very difficult. When you win thirty-six bouquets a year and you've gotten into the habit, twice a week, of giving them to your mother and your friends, it's awful to race three and a half years and not bring home even one bouquet.

"Before this, I used to think of bicycling as something between a religion and a love, but then it became just a profession, a job. Now I take cycling as it comes. Everything goes well—terrific. Things don't go too well—that's okay too. Since I realized that I wasn't going to make it big, bicycling has changed for me. When you've put in ten years with the pros, seen what you've seen, suffered what you've suffered, you can handle the rest of life. The hard knocks and the defeats —I don't care about them, because bicycling has taught me how to live.

"I don't regret anything, understand that. But I would have preferred starting as a pro without ambition. That would have been less difficult. It's hard to have a Mercedes at eighteen and a jalopy at thirty-five. I was at the top and I fell into obscurity."

○

"The first time I was invited to travel with the Tour de France," said a French television personality, one of those people some teams bring along in their cars as official guests, "it was in the Pyrenees, and in the fog and rain we came to a spill of about thirty riders. They were lying all over the road. We drove on, and a little while later we were having our lunch in the car—chicken, wine, strawberries—when some of the men in the crash went by and I saw them through the windows, covered with rain, and with blood streaming down their faces. I was having lunch and I was embarrassed, so I rolled down the window and told one of them I was sorry. And he just said, 'It's okay, I'm used to it.'"

○

This morning in early March, Paris scents spring. Winter is not joyful here: when the gray months start in November, there is no sun, and the blue sky the Impressionists painted, darkened for decades by automobile exhaust fumes, turns gloomier still. An hour away from the great bowl that is Paris, in the bean fields of Arpajon or on the grape hills of Champagne, there may be snow. But in the city the rare snowfall melts quickly in the streets. It is cold but never cold enough for winter to assert itself. In Paris, winter is a negative season, and the cheerless months follow each other like doughboys in a World War I photograph, shuffling to the front as the mud sucks at their boots and the rain turns their greatcoats black.

Spring is another parade altogether, royal blue and starched tan, the golden braid and crimson piping of soldiers stepping smartly down the Champs-Elysées. Spring is a military band playing a march scored for cymbals. But this March morning, when the forsythia is just beginning to open, the marchers are in business suits and white aprons. At the Place de la Bastille, thousands of small businessmen shuffle along under banners protesting the rate of inflation, then near 10 percent despite official promises. In two days the steelworkers of Lorraine and Flanders will march the same route, eyed by the same riot policemen, to protest the government's decision to close their mills, which are no longer competitive on the world market. Next week government employees will parade to protest a plan to force them to contribute to the social security system.

There is also music: from the Hôtel de Ville, the city hall, come the sounds of an accordion. A wind from the nearby Seine carries the tune around the plaza: the upbeat "Viva España," the traditional French introduction to anything Spanish. While a crowd of several hundred looks on, the Teka professional bicycle team rolls past wooden barricades and into the plaza. Far from base in sunny Valencia ("In my dreams, I hear you calling me"), the Spanish riders look cold. They wear long leggings and heavy jerseys, and in semblance of warmth have pulled their cloth caps low over their eyes, but not low enough to hide their expressions. They look dubious as they park their bicycles and file into the city hall.

The accordion turns to "La Vie en Rose" to welcome the next riders, the pink-shirted Système U team. Each of the seventeen teams arrives to a song or even a medley, depending on how strung out are its riders, up to ten a team. Each team wins a round of applause from the crowd, mostly businessmen and the obviously retired, many of them in the beret that only country people wear now. Paris draws them, in their old age, to live with the children who long ago left their native villages; the sons are in business suits, but the fathers still wear the beret or the distinctive Breton sweater. A group of tourists hurry by to the Pompidou Center, quickly losing interest at the sight of bicycles: "They look a bit lost, set down / In this unamerican place," Auden wrote in "Fleet Visit," understanding that, "One baseball game is more / To them than fifty Troys." Soon the mayor will arrive and make a short speech on the outdoor podium, wishing all the riders well in the Paris-Nice race. He goes on a bit too long, but few in the audience begin drifting away for lunch. The riders also stay put. The speeches and ceremonial welcome are part of their job, like the compulsory round of handshaking with which the French worker warmly greets colleagues he has not seen for the twelve hours since he shook their hands to say goodbye. The music, the speeches, the standing around in the cold—all this a rite of spring.

○

During the winter the cycling columns of the daily sports newspaper *L'Equipe* have been full of gossip, for want of anything better: this rider is changing teams, that rider is planning a comeback; this team manager is revealing his hopes for the coming season, that manager is already preparing his excuses. Some of the riders have spent a week in Senegal or Martinique, racing when not basking in the sun. The gossip is hospital food, nourishing but thin. Then the first crocus pushes through the snow. The Coop team has gathered in the Alps for an oxygenation stage—bicycle racers believe mightily in the power of clear air to reinvigorate the body—and will shortly start training on the road. Soon begin some of the innumerable and unimportant short races that are a specialty on the Riviera, or Côte d'Azur, in February. Along the coast from Monaco to Cannes and back in the hills, where a soft wind stirs, the riders will resume climbing and descending, leaning into curves shielded by palm trees.

Most of these races last a day, and the more important ones are called classics. They ease the riders into the longer races, the ones run in daily stages, of which Paris-Nice is always the year's first major one. In a half hour the riders will get back on their bicycles and pedal slowly to the suburbs, where they will begin their weeklong race to the Côte d'Azur. Down there the mimosa is in flower, and some afternoons it is already hot enough to raise the scent of lavender off the hills along the road. There are snowy mountain passes to cross first and sleet storms to endure, but the season has opened and spring is officially on the way. All through the bleak winter the bicycling magazines have published the classic photograph of professional racing: in soft focus in the foreground a field of poppies or bachelor's buttons or daffodils, and behind the flowers the riders in their short-sleeved jerseys. The yellow of Renault-Elf reflects the daffodils, the scarlet slashes of Skil-Sem highlight the poppies, and the blue of La Redoute the bachelor's buttons.

Sitting upright and relaxed in the photograph, the riders are obviously on a flat stretch and nobody is yet trying to break away or otherwise disturb the torpor of a day in the country, cruising for 7 or 8 hours at a speed of 35 kilometers an hour, a bit over 20 miles an hour. Most of the riders are staring ahead, but a few are looking around, checking a rival's position or seeking a friend. Nobody is admiring the scenery, although some riders say that on a long and slow uphill they do notice the cows in the fields or the roadside crops. It depends on the rider: a former farmboy will be interested in the height of the field corn, while a rider from the coal-mining north may just marvel at how small are the parcels of land into which a farm has been subdivided among sons.

In the photograph some mouths are open and the conversation must be banal: like workers anywhere, the riders say they discuss women and politics and their dumb employers.

Money is never discussed, they say; professional bicycle racing is a badly paid sport, and nobody likes to admit his distress. Even after the Socialist government's efforts to raise the monthly minimum wage, it was still just under 4,000 francs (less than $450) a month for a worker in 1984. This figure is known as the SMIC (from *salaire minimum interprofessionnel de croissance*), and many racers are Smicards or only a bit better. In a poll taken in 1983 by the magazine *Miroir du Cyclisme,* 50 percent of the French *peloton*—the pack, about one hundred professional riders employed by teams—said they were paid up to 4,500 francs a month. Twenty-two percent more were paid up to 6,500 francs and only 10 percent were paid at least 10,000 francs. Team leaders are paid considerably more, of course, with a star earning about $75,000 to $100,000 a year and a superstar twice or three times that, not including the rare endorsement or bonus.

For the average racer, there are a few ways to augment his income. He can win a race prize, although these are often derisory, ranging around the $1,500 given to the winner of, for example, the Paris-Roubaix classic, a race so trying that it is nicknamed the Hell of the North. Or the average rider can share in the prizes that his leader wins and, by tradition, turns over to the team pool. Finally there are the critériums and kermesses—country-fair types of one-day races to which admission is charged, unlike the usual bicycle race, which is free along the public highways. For the critériums and kermesses, which proliferate after the Tour de France in July, the riders are paid an appearance fee varying with the gate appeal of their names. Here is Bernard Vallet of the Vie Claire team on the value of the best climber's jersey—white with red polka dots—in the Tour de France: "My manager let me know that if I kept the jersey to Paris, my name goes first on the posters for some critériums and my fee, usually about twenty-five hundred francs, can go to between forty-five hundred and six thousand. That's what the jersey's worth—just about double."

The magazine survey of French riders showed how hard their life is. Nearly half reported they covered between 20,000 and 30,000 kilometers (12,500 to 18,750 miles)* a year just in training, including both team rides during the season and solitary rides during the winter. Sixty percent estimated they spent between 15 and 25 hours a week in training, with 25 percent saying they spent between 30 and 35 hours. Nearly half reported they had covered from 35,000 to more than 50,000 kilometers a year by car, traveling to and from races and critériums; this is an especially trying time for riders, who complain that their muscles cramp in a car.

Complaints about the competitive calendar are widespread, with 80 percent of the riders voicing unhappiness: the season lasts too many months, the races are too numerous and too close together and too long. (There are a third more races now than in the 1960s, when the sport was generally considered to be in a golden age of popularity.) Nearly half say they spend no more than four days a month at home during the season. More demographics: Each year the turnover rate—new professionals and transfers among teams—in the French *peloton* is nearly 25 percent; nearly half the riders in the survey have only a one-year team contract, nearly 90 percent have ridden for one team or no more than two, and 75 percent are in no more than their third year as a professional. More than half began as amateurs at age fourteen or fifteen, with 97 percent of their families approving, and few earned high-school diplomas. Most riders turn professional at twenty-one or twenty-two, and most are gone from the sport before thirty. Sixty percent worry about their future when their racing days are over, with nearly three quarters not yet even sure what they will do; a common occupation is running a small bicycle or sporting-goods shop in their hometowns.

Underpaid, overused, rarely with their families, and worried about the future—why do they race? Listen to Marc Madiot, a young rider with the Renault team: "When you choose to become a professional, you have to be young and either naïve or a megalomaniac. As for me, I was young, just seventeen, naïve and, most of all, crazy about cycling."

Amoureux fou du vélo, crazy about cycling. Fifty-nine percent of the riders listed love of the sport as the main reason they turned professional. Twenty-nine percent more listed it as second choice. Fifteen

*1 kilometer = 0.6214 mile.

percent primarily sought glory, 12 percent turned to the sport for the money, and 3 percent for social mobility, a way up from the farm in Brittany or steel mill in Picardy or shoe factory in Burgundy. A whopping 50 percent chose social mobility as their second or third reason to turn professional.

Pascal Jules of the Renault team on why he became a racer after working three years as a mason's assistant: "I carried water for them, fifty-kilogram buckets, and got home every night exhausted and with bloody shoulders. I understood that I had to find another way." But as France becomes less a country of class extremes, the craving for social mobility lessens, too—or so it seems to some veterans. Bernard Thévenet, the thirty-seven-year-old manager of La Redoute's team and a two-time winner of the Tour de France, says, "For our generation, cycling was a way upward. We were more motivated to make the sacrifices cycling demands. Money came later. Now it seems that some riders want everything at once. That's impossible."

○

At the Hôtel de Ville in Paris, the politicians' speeches have ended. More than one has pointed to the Paris-Nice race as a sign that despite the protests in the streets France is still France; when the Tour was in doubt during the student and worker upheavals of May 1968, the government ordered the race to be held as a sign to the world that all was really well.

Walking daintily in racing shoes with turned-up tips to hold better in the wire traps over the pedals, the riders get on their bicycles and begin moving out. A cloud has come over the sun. In the next few weeks the newspapers and bicycle magazines will show race photographs of Jean-Luc Vandenbroucke, a Belgian rider, with hands swollen and frozen; of Jean-Claude Bagot, a French rider, heading on a breakaway into a wall of fog; of Stephen Roche, an Irish rider, grimacing with pain after a mountain finish under rain and sleet. Bernard Hinault, the French star and four-time winner of the Tour de France, will report two fingers still partly frozen a week after a climb through the Massif Central. This morning in early March, Paris has scented spring, but first there are races to be run. The way to the mimosa on the Côte d'Azur is over mountain passes lined with snow. The time of year is not spring—not yet—but bicycle season.

Many countries have bicycling tours,

among them Italy, Spain, the Netherlands, Luxembourg, Switzerland, Britain, Colombia, Sweden, Morocco, Norway, Portugal, and sometimes Belgium and the United States. Martinique has a tour and so does the Ivory Coast. Eastern Europe has what amounts to a tour of Poland, Czechoslovakia, and East Germany, called the Peace Race. Some of these tours, like the ones in Sweden and Britain, attract mainly amateur riders and are thus unimportant to professional teams. Others, like those in Martinique and the Ivory Coast, are unimportant because they are held after the European season and thus become only a way of paying for a vacation in the sun. Because of geography, some tours are short—none of the Benelux tours can be stretched into more than three days—and unimportant. Others can last a week longer, like the Tour of Switzerland, and not be much more important because they are primarily tune-up races for a bigger tour. The tours that matter are those of Spain, Italy, and France, which are held in that chronological order in the spring and summer, and of these, the Tour de France is supreme.

The three all last about the same time, nearly three weeks, and cover about the same distance, close to 4,000 kilometers, but nobody quarrels with the judgment of Modesto Urrutibeazcoa, a Spaniard who rides for the Teka team and said of the French race: "It's the center of the season. All our work is for this." Or with the opinion of Angel Arroyo, another Spaniard, who finished second while riding for the Reynolds team in 1983 and spent the next year preparing for another chance: "The Tour de France is the greatest race in the world. It's well worth sacrificing twelve months of your life for." Nobody can miss the meaning of the words of Ferdinand Julien, who rode during the 1970s:

"When I became a professional, I dreamed, of course, about riding in the Tour de France. And now look: I'm there. Nobody ever helped me. Even my parents were against my becoming a pro. And I'm there. You understand: I'm there."

What sets the Tour de France apart? For one thing, money. Its overall prizes exceed 2.5 million francs (about $250,000, depending on the strength of the dollar against the depleted franc). For another thing, size. The Tour de France is virtually a sovereign state, complete with its own motorcycle police force (members of the Garde Républicaine from Paris), its own traveling bank (the only one open in France on Bastille Day, July 14), and more than 2,000 full-time subjects (the 170-odd riders are far outnumbered by reporters, photographers, team officials, mechanics, masseurs, chauffeurs, judges, and salesmen).

For a third difference, prestige. The world championship, held every year early in September, is a fine race to win, but as Allan Peiper, an Australian with the Peugeot team, said of the Tour de France in 1984, "This is the real world championship. The other just shows who's best for one day." And for a fourth distinction, seriousness. The Tour of Spain, the Vuelta, rarely attracts top teams from outside that country, where bicycle racing has been in the doldrums for more than a decade.

The Tour of Italy, the Giro, is the only rival to the Tour de France, but the Giro is hard to take seriously: when the Italians are not giving slivers of saints' bones as bonuses instead of money, they cheat. The Italian public wants Italian riders to win, and the Italian organizers are remarkably responsive to this national yearning. To assist an Italian rider who was certain to collapse in the Alps, the organizers eliminated the highest mountain stage in 1984, insisting that the pass was snowbound and producing photographs of arctic scenes that would have intimidated Nanook of the North. When curious French team officials visited the pass, it was open and lined with no more snow than the Tour de France sees on any summer day in its Alps.

Moreover, Italian bicycle fans, like those in Spain, can be vicious to foreigners. The Spanish often spit on a visiting rider or try to punch him off his bicycle if he is leading their tour; on a hot day, when fans in other countries pour water over a struggling rider, the Italians have been known to douse a foreigner with vinegar. French fans are better behaved by far, and rarely is there an incident like the day in 1975 when a Frenchman slugged Eddy Merckx, a Belgian, as he labored uphill unsuccessfully seeking his sixth victory in the Tour de France.

The riders appreciate the attitude of the French fans. "The trouble here," said Barry Hoban, an English rider, in the Netherlands before the start of the 1978 Tour de France, "is that they don't know what to make of racers. They don't really understand the Tour de France, and that's rubbed off on all of us.

"But when we get to France," he said, brightening, "ah, there they know how to make a racer feel important."

One way the French do this is by turning out in vast numbers to watch the passing parade. More than a third of the country's 55 million people, 20 million in all, are estimated to line the sides of the Tour's road, which is closed to all other traffic for 90 minutes before the race comes through and 10 minutes afterward. On the flat, a spectator can expect to see a few moments' worth of the bicyclists, preceded and followed by a retinue using all known modes of conveyance except bicycles. ("On a bike, that's the only way to do the Tour de France," Greg LeMond, an American rider, insisted. "Sitting in a car all your muscles get cramped. On a bicycle, you stay loose." Probably he was joking.)

In the mountains the pack tends to string out as it moves slowly uphill, and so the view of the race lasts longer. Families bring picnic lunches and make a day of it. At some climbs, like the one at L'Alpe-d'Huez, hundreds of thousands park along the hairpin turns that ascend for 12 kilometers, and many of them arrive the day before the riders to assure themselves of the right vantage point.

These fans all could have seen the race better and more comfortably on a television set, since every finish of the daily stages is shown live in Western Europe. The French also offer a 15-minute televised recap each evening, plus live coverage, on some radio stations, of parts of major stages. Newspapers are full of articles about the Tour before, during, and after its run, with important results often on page one. Commentaries and lists of standings fill inside pages, with provincial papers in bicycle-mad Brittany, for example, devoting three and four pages daily to the race, as does the national sports newspaper *L'Equipe.*

Newsstands display almost as many magazines devoted to professional cycling as to food and wine, photographs of French riders hang in many store windows and banners line the route, which is often painted with the name of a rider and the exhortatory "*Allez*"—go.

The Tour de France is the center of French life in July. Why this is so has been the subject of learned discussion for years, but the best explanation may be, as has often been remarked, that the French love sports, especially played by somebody else. They also love a spectacle and a free outing, which the barnstorming Tour offers daily.

A few years back, there were fears that the Tour was losing some popularity because of its long traditions, that it was regarded as something from grandfather's time: *rétro,* not *moderne.* To counter this image, the organizers for the first time invited amateur teams in 1983, although European professionals dispute the amateur standing of Eastern Europeans, Colombians, and other state-supported cyclists. Because of their relative lack of experience and toughness, the amateurs were not an important factor. No matter, the Tour was altering its format.

Soccer's World Cup in Spain in 1982, which attracted an enormous television following amid a circus of hucksterism, showed how vast the market for sports is in the summertime, when most Europeans have at least four weeks off. The Tour de France learned to think bigger. Now the organizers were talking of further changes, including an expansion into a Tour of the World, with stages in the United States and Eastern Europe. Also under study was a return to national teams instead of ones sponsored by manufacturers of ice cream, furniture, trucks, cars, and garden equipment. The riders might protest the proposed changes, the sponsors might threaten to sue, but the polls showed that the public approved.

Nostalgia isn't what it used to be, at least what it was back in 1903, when Géo Lefèvre, the cycling correspondent for the newspaper *L'Auto,* thought of the idea for a long race, and his editor, Henri Desgrange, seized it and organized the first Tour. Desgrange thought of the race as a circulation builder, which it still is; *L'Equipe,* the descendant of *L'Auto* and one of the two organizers of the race, says its usual daily circulation of 290,000 rises to 400,000 during July, when it sends about fifteen reporters and photographers into the field. *Parisien Libéré,* the other sponsoring newspaper, says its circulation rises about 10 percent above its usual 375,000.

At the time of the first Tour de France intercity bicycle races had been popular for decades, with the first, Paris-Rouen, run in 1869, more than a year after the first recorded bicycle race, which was held in the Paris suburb of Saint-Cloud. Such enduring races as Bordeaux-Paris, Paris-Roubaix, and Liège-Bastogne-Liège started before the turn of the century, but what Desgrange devised was a continuing race, not a one-day classic. For that first race Desgrange developed the formula that still governs: a series of daily stages run during three weeks in July with the overall winner decided on the basis of overall accumulated time. Sixty riders turned out for the first Tour de France, which covered 2,428 kilometers in six stages, both day and night, Paris-Lyon, Lyon-Marseille, Marseille-Toulouse, Toulouse-Bordeaux, Bordeaux-Nantes, and Nantes-Paris.

All went well the first time, with the thirty-two-year-old Maurice Garin winning by 2 hours 49 minutes and taking the first prize of 6,125 gold francs out of 20,000 offered. Happily for Desgrange and his newspaper, Garin was the stuff of legend, a native-born Italian who had come to France as a boy and was traded by his father to a chimney sweep in Savoie for a wheel of cheese. "The Little Chimney Sweep," Desgrange dubbed him, the first in a line of Giants of the Road, as *L'Equipe* sometimes still calls riders.

The new race suffered a setback in 1904, when crowds of toughs blocked the roads during night courses, beating some riders and allowing their favorites through. Then, four months after the finish, the first four leaders, including Garin, were disqualified for irregularities that were never made public but presumably included traveling by car. Although Desgrange announced that the race was finished, it was held again in 1905 and has been every year since except during both world wars. The 1984 Tour was the seventy-first.

Bit by bit in the early years the race was being set in its present form. In 1905 the night courses were eliminated, the race lengthened by 500 kilometers, and the first mountain, the Ballon d'Alsace, added. In 1907 bicycle manufacturers other than Peugeot, which had a monopoly, were allowed to sponsor riders, and team cars were given the right to follow closely. The geographical structure was also being decided, with the Alps, the Pyrenees, the Massif Central, and Paris the cornerstones of the trip, either clockwise or counterclockwise, around France; the specific route changes every year.

The lore of the Tour de France was also building; there were two tales they still tell. The first dates from 1910, with the first climb in the Pyrenees, then mountains better fit for bears and shepherds. Desgrange, who was busy forging heroes, approved the climb through the 1,700-meter-high Col d'Aubisque, although an agent reported that the road up to the pass was no more than a mule track. On the day of the race, the editor waited with other officials at the bottom of the mountain for hours past the expected arrival of the racers. Finally one appeared, but could not or would not speak. Then Octave Lapize, the race's leader, made his way down, stared at Desgrange, and spat out the word, "Assassin." According to all accounts, Desgrange was pleased.

The other story tells of Eugène Christophe, who broke the front fork of his bicycle while descending, in second place, from the Tourmalet pass in the Pyrenees during the 1913 race. As the rules specified, he had to repair his bicycle himself, so he picked it up and walked 10 kilometers to the nearest village, where he found a blacksmith's shop and proceeded to forge the needed piece. The work went on for four hours while the officials who were overseeing his labor began to fidget with hunger. "Have *I* eaten?" cried Christophe.

Finished at last, he rode on to rejoin the Tour. A plaque in the village of Sainte-Marie-de-Campan still marks the former blacksmith's shop. The plaque does not report what some history books do: shortly after catching up to the main body of riders, Christophe learned that he had been penalized an additional three minutes for having allowed a small boy to work the bellows while he had both hands full hammering the new fork.

○

Despite the efforts of the Socialist government to decentralize France, Paris remains as the fabulist La Fontaine saw it in the seventeenth century: "This great city . . . the glory of France." Sometimes, though, the glory is shared. The window of a beauty parlor in Fleurance, a sleepy town in the southwest, was once drawn over in lipstick with a map of France. Only two places were identified: Fleurance, where that year's Tour de France began, and Paris, where it ended.

Not often are these two municipalities paired, but for a few days before the start of the race, the map was valid. The Tour does that for a small town, gives it a touch of importance, an international dateline, a place on European television, including, at the end of each day's program, a 30-second panoramic picture from a helicopter. Suddenly the world has heard of Fleurance or Luchon or Saint-Brieuc or any of the other corners where the racers stop for the night.

It is in these small towns, which annually replace one another on the Tour's map, that the riders are most fussed over. Shops, even banks, close because the residents are thronging the arrival and departure areas to inspect the bicycles and their riders. In the evening, when a day's racing stage is done, the welcome can be brisk. The riders sprint past the finish, push through the crowds, leave their bicycles with a mechanic, and vanish in their team cars. The best a fan can do is perhaps touch a bicycle as it is wheeled away, or watch as the day's winner receives the inevitable kiss and flowers wrapped in cellophane.

But each morning, in the half hour before the departure for another stage in the race, riders and the public meet. Old men turn up in full racing regalia to glide on their bicycles among the riders, mimicking youth's pursuit. The police are notably lenient about letting young children wander around asking for autographs. If they are feeling any tension, the riders disguise it by chatting with their fans.

Then whistles blow and the riders gather on their bicycles. The real start usually takes place outside town, on an otherwise empty road, but the Tour likes to pretend—just one more time each day—that the town it is visiting is really the focus of the race. The signal is given and the riders move out. Down the street they go, around a corner, and then they are gone. For a few minutes the town seems empty, but down the road lie other towns waiting for a few hours of recognition.

For a price, a town can buy a few days of recognition by sponsoring the start of the entire race, which entitles it to two full days and the succeeding morning of activity. Because the price is so high, roughly half a million dollars, the Tour de France sometimes starts in one of Europe's major cities—in Frankfurt in 1980, in Nice in 1981, in Basel in 1982, although not in Paris in the last thirty years. In the hard times of the early-1980s, the organizers of the race came up with the notion of not just a city or a town as the sponsor but an entire region. The start in 1983 was in the Val-de-Marne Department, southeast of Paris, and in 1984 it was in the Seine-Saint-Denis Department, north of the capital, those suburbs just beyond the city limits that used to be known as the Red Belt because of the postwar influx of workers with Communist voting patterns. Towns that had been farming centers for centuries were planted with factories and cheap skyscraper housing, known as HLM (from *habitation à loyer modéré,* or low-rent housing). In some cases, World War II made the job easier: Noisy-le-Sec, which was awarded the Croix de Guerre after it was destroyed in air raids in 1944 and declared a dead city by the government, was rebuilt and studded with HLMs.

In the Val-de-Marne Department, barely 25 minutes from the Bastille métro station, the race was spread over more than twenty municipalities, but the center of activity was Créteil, a new town of high-rise buildings with landscaped walks around a lake. By long-standing government policy, the flight to the suburbs is not by the French middle class, which stays rooted in Paris, but by the working class or those a rung above it. Créteil, the administrative capital of Val-de-Marne, is also its showpiece, its buildings varied architecturally and marked by panels of bright color. During lunch, children leave their bicycles unlocked outside. Bluebells, bachelor's buttons, honeysuckle, and puffy pink roses line the town's walks, and small sailboats and windsurfers dot the lake. Manners count: at the subway station, the most that a young Val-de-Marne punk, with waxed upright hair and a heavy chain necklace, will do to show his disdain is strut into the first-class métro car with a second-class ticket.

Seine-Saint-Denis is a tougher place, with some of its towns no better than squalid. A few are heard of only during the summer, when the torpor seems annually to drive somebody to fire a few shots from a seventeenth-floor apartment at the group of North African children playing noisily on the dusty patch that was designed as a front lawn. One in eight persons living in France is an immigrant these days, usually from North Africa or the many sub-Saharan countries that were once part of the French empire: distant lands like Mali, Chad, Cameroon, or Upper Volta, which supply the street sweepers and manual laborers for the jobs the true French will no longer accept. In Seine-Saint-Denis, the proportion of immigrants is far higher than one in eight, and the streets and métros are filled mainly with blacks. Tensions rise: this may be the Red Belt, but nearly 16 percent, almost double the national average, voted for the far-right National Front in the 1984 elections for a European parliament.

White or black, life here seems joyless. Saint-Ouen, a town in the Red Belt, is habitually the locus in French movies about the ex-convict who finds life hard outside the walls and can only return to hanging out in the same bars and dark apartments he came from. The tourists' flea market, the Marché aux Puces, is in Saint-Ouen, and it was there that the police went the day after eighteen bicycles were stolen from a truck while the Redoute team was having dinner before the 1984 Tour. The riders were spread out through many towns in the area, and reports of burglaries of hotel rooms were frequent.

Class struggle is alive here, fanned by even the street names—the ubiquitous Avenue Stalingrad, Place Salvador Allende, Boulevard Maurice Thorez, Lycée Léon Blum. In Montreuil there is a nursery named to honor Valentina Tereshkova, the Soviet cosmonaut, and in Bobigny a social-service center is named in honor of a Curie, neither Pierre nor Marie, the discoverers of radium, but Jean Frédéric Joliot-Curie, the political activist. Again in Bobigny, the 1885 town hall, now superseded by an all-glass skyscraper a quarter of a mile away, has a side yard with a plinth of Lenin and a praiseful quote from Gorky. The Rue Maxime Gorky is another favorite in the Red Belt. In Stains, a banner at the town hall advertised a day of solidarity with Nicaragua.

These are towns of shopping centers, replacing the traditional French small stores. Nothing is stale in the shopping-center bakery, which advertises deliveries three times a day, but the pastries are tasteless. Office workers are dowdy, with none of the chic dress or makeup seen in Paris, nearly as far away as Nicaragua.

Bicycle racing is popular among the people who live in Seine-Saint-Denis, which is why the regional government said it bid for the start of the Tour. This seemed to be the commendable truth. There was a noted lack of the local boosterism that marked other starts but, as the cynics said, what could Seine-Saint-Denis possibly try to sell except for the stolen La Redoute bicycles?

THREE

"*There is a saying here,*" *Red Smith* wrote from France in 1960, "that an army from Mars could invade France, the government could fall, and even the recipe for sauce Béarnaise be lost, but if it happened during the Tour de France, nobody would notice." In the years since this observation, governments—though not the Martians—have come and gone and the tarragon-flavored sauce has become available in any grocery store frozen, bottled, and canned. But a few years ago the Tour began escaping Frenchmen's notice.

The trouble was that the French did not particularly like Bernard Hinault, a Breton who had won the Tour de France four times since his debut in 1978. Though widely repected, Hinault was no longer a national hero, a condition he shrugged off with the seeming coldness that cost him much of his public. "I race to win," he has said, "not to please people." He has succeeded at both. "I'm the one who rides," he has insisted. "If somebody thinks he can do it better, let him get a bicycle."

Hinault's domination had reduced the uncertainty about the Tour's outcome to the point where he could say in 1982, "It's a race for second place," and nobody could disagree. The crowds came in diminished numbers and enthusiasm, and even in victory, Hinault was criticized. It was difficult to remember by then how fiery the love affair had been when it began.

After his first victory in the Tour, he was the great hope of French bicycling, if not all sports, so the stories about him found eager listeners. Raymond Poulidor, fourteen times a rider in the Tour but never a winner, told one often in 1978, that first year: "One understood immediately that he had character and that neither Merckx nor Poulidor impressed him. He was afraid of nothing. One day, in the Midi Libre race, I believe, we had a start that went up a mountain. The evening before, Hinault had been hopelessly outdistanced and was, for all practical purposes, out of the race.

"But the next morning he started at full speed and stayed at the head of the pack for twenty-five kilometers, going all out. Behind him we had our hands full to keep up. And then, having done it and showed us, he dropped out of the race. I realized then that we were going to have further dealings with him, that he was not an ordinary racer."

Or Raymond Martin, then riding with the Mercier team: "One time, when he was just starting, during a critérium at Châteaulin, all the big names were there. They were willing to cut me in on the sharing of the prizes, but not him. He got on their nerves too much. So Hinault got mad. He won the first five or six cash bonuses and, if this wasn't bad enough, made faces at the other riders when he swept by them. I told him to cool it, but he replied, 'I don't give a damn.' Totally relaxed. By the seventh or eighth lap, Eddy Merckx came up alongside him and said, 'Okay, you're in on the split, but stop your crap.' "

Luis Ocaña, the 1973 winner of the Tour de France, added to the budding legend: "I remember a stage in the Dauphiné Libéré, it must have been 1975 or 1976. Everybody was calm and the pack was rolling quietly when we got to a long hill. Hinault went to the front and began to ride like a madman. I moved up to him to make him understand that this wasn't on, that he should leave the rest of us in peace.

"Instead of calming down, he just accelerated. We were going all out and soon were exhausted. I dropped back, but he just pushed on. The more everybody yelled at us from behind, the faster he went. He didn't care at all what everybody thought of him, this kid. I liked him at once."

As Poulidor did, the French call this character, a trait they revere —up to a point.

In a few more years they had decided that the stories proved only that Hinault had too much character, and the times called for something different. Ironically, in many ways Hinault was the Frenchman of the 1980s: practical, efficient, and realistic—in short, a pragmatist, or trying hard to be one. Nowadays, nobody talks about *la gloire,* the cornerstone of De Gaullian France, but about inflation and budget deficits and the balance of trade. The franc has been a sick currency for most of the decade, and unemployment was nearly triple the 1 million figure that once was regarded as unacceptable. Projections showed that by 1985 one Frenchman in nine would be on welfare, unemployed, or retired early. What the country needed in its heroes was bravado, gallantry, flare—panache.

Hinault was irritated with complaints that he had shown little panache, a quality the French have come to associate with Tour de France winners. "For me," Hinault said, "panache isn't worth anything. If I go all out in the mountains and then have nothing left the next few days and lose the Tour de France, who really won in the mountains? In the Tour, there are days when you have to know how to win, days when you have to know how to lose, and days when you have to know how to help your opponent, the better to beat him tomorrow. I know all these."

He knows much more. Sitting in the living room of his modern, two-story stone house in Quessoy, a village in Brittany, he sounded like a Ministry of Trade official as he discussed the value of bicycle racing in relation to national exports. When Hinault's sponsor was Renault, the French car manufacturer, he raced periodically in such big foreign markets as Italy and Spain. He wanted badly to ride in the first Tour of America in 1982—a three-day race through Virginia and the District of Columbia—but could not get permission from the organizers of a simultaneous race in France that had first call on his services. As a pragmatist, he was peeved. "France is a country that needs exports," he explained, "and for Renault, this includes the car we are building in the United States. Appearing in a bicycle race is one way of advertising, not only Renault but also Gitane"—then Hinault's secondary sponsor and Renault's bicycle-making subsidiary. Up to 100 million bicycles are manufactured worldwide each year, with China accounting for 20 million, the United States and Japan tied for second, with about 10 million each, and France far behind, with under 2 million. Even at home, French bicycle manufacturers' share of the market fell from 78 percent to 70 percent in the five years up to 1983.

Hinault gave practiced answers to cycling questions, but really came alive when he talked about what was occupying the thoughts of his countrymen. He grumped about unemployment benefits ("Everywhere in France now you see people begging for money, and everywhere you see jobs begging for people") and taxes ("If I push the pedal five times, one is for me and my family and four are for the tax collector"). With an annual income estimated between $300,000 and $500,000, including salary, prizes, endorsements, and bonuses, he is rare in cycling circles for having a professional business manager. Still, like everybody else, he brooded about his future. "For racing, nature gives you certain gifts, but for retirement, nature gives you nothing. It's up to you to arrange it. If I'm a failure in retiring, then my whole career will have meant nothing."

Hinault insisted he would retire in 1986, and he had already bought a farm—65 kilometers from Quessoy, but still in Brittany—where he intends to move with his wife and two small sons to raise dairy cattle and become, as he put it, a peasant. The son of a railroad worker in the nearby town of Yffiniac, he seems to many Frenchmen the definitive Breton, right down to his Celtic dark good looks. However, most Frenchmen do not think of these as the chief Breton trait. Instead, "stubborn as a Breton" is a common epithet.

"People say that Bretons have a hard character, stubborn, even rude," said Martine Hinault as she waited for her husband to complete a training run over flat, windblown roads. "That's our reputation—aggressive and stubborn."

When he returned home, Hinault flopped onto the couch and politely differed. "I think it refers to people who are hard, who are able to endure bad climate, among other things. I think when people refer to the Breton character, they mean people who when they want something do their best to get it."

This definition was tidy and, in Hinault's case, the truth—but not the whole truth. Vividly remembered was the tantrum he threw in 1982 when, a beaten man, he dropped out of the one-day French championship and then, on nationwide television, blamed the public, the press, and his fellow riders. The other bicyclists kept a politic silence, but the public responded throughout the Tour de France with jeers and whistles. The press let loose with long-suppressed anger. "A small masterpiece of the hateful and the stupid," said *L'Equipe* of Hinault's petulance. "In the eyes of the general public, Bernard Hinault is revealed for what he is: a great champion but a small man."

23

"My nature isn't always to be prudent," said Hinault, responding to the editorial. "As everybody knows, I can sometimes be impulsive." He laughed at his statement of the obvious.

Another word usually attached to Hinault was *méchant,* literally meaning spiteful, nasty, or malicious. French homes often have signs warning of a *chien méchant,* a vicious dog. In cycling, to be *méchant* is not to be all bad, as Hinault noted. "It's natural for a cyclist to be *méchant,"* he said, "I can't understand how a racer cannot have this trait, at least a bit of it. All winners have it. People who like to fight, who like to win, they all have it. I think when you're going all out, it's impossible to do it with a smile. If you ever see me smiling during a race, you'll know I'm not really competing." Hinault's standard race photograph shows glaring, burning eyes and a set jaw. He resembles an animal on the scent and is, indeed, nicknamed for one—*le blaireau,* the badger.

Hinault rose from the couch and crossed the room to display a stuffed and mounted badger, teeth bared, that a fan had sent. "The nickname was given to me by another rider early in my career, and it stuck. The badger is a strong animal, especially in relation to its small size, and he can make a lot of trouble if he's attacked. I think the nickname sort of reflects my own attitude: I can take a lot of blows without saying anything, but the next day I attack, and when I do, I can be very, very *méchant."* Hinault glared at the badger, then grinned.

A French bicycle fan was troubled a few years ago when he wrote a letter to *L'Equipe*: "We Frenchmen have Bernard Hinault, and we don't have the right to complain about him. We should be proud of him. It's worth more to have several French victories of five or six minutes each than one French victory of forty-five minutes every fifteen years. If the winner of the Tour de France had been a foreigner, it would be the same Frenchmen who would be complaining."

Hinault agreed with the tactical sense of the letter, although not with the chauvinism. He welcomed the growing popularity of bicycling abroad and, while still with Renault, designated as his cycling heir a young American, Greg LeMond, who became his teammate in 1980. "It doesn't bother me at all that he's not French. If the French want to catch up to him, let them make the effort."

The pragmatist continued: "What good are legends?" he asked.

"What good does it do if I win the Tour de France by ten or fifteen minutes instead of six? I race to last, not to finish broken."

Hinault worries about lasting. "When I first started in the Tour, in 1978, I showed a bit of the spirit of youth, superior physical strength. Now I'm more calculating, more a thinking rider. When I look around, I don't see many riders left who started with me."

Like being *méchant*, calculation can be a strength in a bicyclist. "To win the Tour de France," Hinault explained, leaning forward to give his words weight, "you've got to do well in everything—be able to win in the mountains when you must, win a time trial, or at least do well. It's enough to be a champion in one discipline if you're good enough in the others, a complete athlete. You can't win the Tour if you have any weaknesses." A strong climber, he had long excelled in time trials, individual races against the clock over distances ranging from 8 to 60 kilometers. Four or five are held each Tour, plus one for teams.

With four victories in the Tour de France, this year Hinault could equal the record of five shared by Jacques Anquetil and Eddy Merckx. Anquetil finished first in 1957 and 1961 through 1964, and Merckx in 1969 through 1972 and 1974. Hinault knew that his time was running out— he would turn thirty in November 1984. "Until the age of thirty," he said, "I don't want to think about anything except bicycle riding, about winning. Starting at thirty, I'll begin to think about other things, including my farm. I want to retire correctly, without bitterness, without feeling bad about leaving racing. After thirty, I'll probably not be as competitive as I am now and so my role will be to give the kids I ride with the best chance to win. I'll be more of a road captain, saying, This is the way you do this, this is the way you do that."

But first he had something to prove. After being forced to withdraw from the 1983 race because of tendinitis in the right knee, he defied most advice and insisted on a quick operation. Then, in a suicide note in the form of a business letter, he forced a showdown with his team over what he perceived as his lack of freedom. He told Renault to choose between him and the team's manager, Cyrille Guimard. Renault chose Guimard, as it had to after two of his racers won the Tour de France and the world championship while Hinault was ailing.

After frenzied offers from Spanish, Italian, Belgian, and French teams, Hinault signed a ten-year personal-services contract with a

French businessman, Bernard Tapie, whose specialty was rescuing companies in distress. The primary sponsor was to be La Vie Claire, a Tapie chain of health-food stores.

Hinault had his explanation for the break with Renault, which he almost always phrased in marital terms: "My divorce is due to the backward character of the world of cycling, in which the rider, who is the key part of the edifice, is systematically kept from making any of the decisions that concern him and is considered simply a mass of muscles with a soul—in short, a child."

Tapie put it another way: "Hinault quit Renault for reasons that can be explained in psychoanalytic terms. It's the famous theme of the son wanting to say 'shit' to his father."

Hinault dedicated the 1984 season to winning the Tour and showing the world: all winter he repeatedly told his critics, "We have an appointment at the Tour de France. We will talk there." He dismissed all questions about his possible decline, much debated after his knee operation was followed by weak showings in the spring. Anquetil, now a wealthy landowner and occasional race commentator, felt Hinault could not stay long at his peak. "When you've been champion six or seven years, you're invariably the victim of a certain lassitude," he explained. "You're able to bring off a coup now and then, but it's nearly impossible to win a long race like the Tour de France. If Hinault has become prudent, it's not just by chance."

"Decline, decline," Hinault responded. "I'd rather think that I'm like a good wine and that I get better as I get older. I think it's fair to say that the Tour has been my race for the last few years. There are some races when I've really prepared for them, that I'm there to win. I simply don't have the right not to win."

○

Greg LeMond turned twenty-three on June 26, 1984, and, as usual, didn't expect much of a celebration. "His birthday is always a dud," his wife, Kathy, said beforehand at their home in Kortrijk, Belgium. One problem was that, as the world professional bicycle-racing champion that year, LeMond would be away from home often during the busy month of June.

He was in fact off racing in the Netherlands that day, although he managed to get home late in the evening. It could have been worse.

"One year we were in Hamburg and the only thing we could do to celebrate was to go to a fast-food place, have two or three beers, and then go back to our hotel to sleep," he recalled.

So LeMond has learned to be low-key about his birthday. Gravely, he even refused to say that a special present he could give himself might be a victory in the Tour de France, which would begin three days after his birthday. Although this was his debut in the Tour, the American rider was one of a handful of favorites.

Aggressive, even fiery, on his bicycle, LeMond is soft-spoken off it. Discussing his chances in the Tour, he started modestly: "I'm going to do as well as I can," he said. "I want to do the best that's possible. If I don't succeed this year, I've got five or six more tries."

He thought about this for a few seconds, then heightened his expectations: "At my age, if I finish in the top three or five, I'll be happy. Not many people win it the first time out, like Hinault or Merckx."

He paused and then his voice grew a shade stronger. "Of course I'm shooting for victory," he admitted. "If you don't, why race at all? You don't ride the Tour de France for the experience."

Leaning back on the living-room couch, LeMond seemed relieved by his confession. Even before he won the world championship and the Super Prestige Pernod award as the season's top-ranked bicyclist in 1983, LeMond, one of two Americans racing then professionally in Europe, learned to deal with his zest for victory. He finished second in the world championship in 1982, leading a final sprint that overtook his fellow American, Jock Boyer, and gave the victory to an Italian, Giuseppe Saronni. Refusing to apologize for possibly depriving Boyer of victory, LeMond voiced regrets only that he had not won himself.

Asked now if he could be happy racing but not winning, he said, "No, probably not. This is my life. I'm doing it to make money for later, and if I don't, then I'm doing it for nothing."

Still, victory seemed not to be absolutely everything to him. He said he much preferred the methods of Bernard Hinault to those of Eddy Merckx, who won five Tours while dominating bicycling a decade before. "Hinault picks his objectives," LeMond explained, "he doesn't try to win everything." Because of his zeal to triumph in every race he entered, Merckx was nicknamed the Cannibal.

"I'm not a cannibal," LeMond said. "In past years, riders sacrificed their health and longevity to win everything, to race from February through October. I think you've got to rest and recuperate between races. I'm not a cannibal because I have a different mentality, maybe because I'm an American."

Being an American in Europe has made many differences for LeMond, a native of Los Angeles who grew up in Nevada, and his wife, a native of La Crosse, Wisconsin. They have lived in Europe since 1980, shortly after they met in her hometown when LeMond trained there with the U.S. team preparing vainly for the Olympic Games in Moscow.

"We decided to get married after we'd known each other only two or three months," Kathy LeMond said. By then, LeMond had also decided that his professional future was in France, where he signed with the Renault team. "My parents thought it was great that we were moving to Europe," she continued. "They had already visited here a lot and really liked it. We go back twice a year and always stop to see my folks and Greg's, so they really see more of us than they see of my brother, who lives in California."

The LeMonds settled first in Nantes, in western France, to be near the manager of the Renault team, Cyrille Guimard. "We lived in Nantes for two years and I saw Guimard maybe once," LeMond recalled. Nantes had other disappointments for him. "I'm still totally American," he said. "I like to go to McDonald's. You can't find one in Nantes. Nantes was totally French. There wasn't even the once-a-week movie in English."

In 1982 the LeMonds moved, first considering Paris but then deciding on Kortrijk, in Belgium. About five miles from the French border, it is a city of 40,000, with a few good restaurants, some picturesque neighborhoods, and a lively street life—the sort of town where the main square is sometimes closed to traffic in the summer so that people can nurse a beer at an outdoor café and listen to a band concert.

Kortrijk had other advantages, the LeMonds felt. "Everybody in Belgium speaks English," he asserted, although his French gets better every year. "My French is funny since I learned it from French racers. I guess I speak the dirtiest language in the world. But it's still hard with the language barrier on the team." The language of Kortrijk is Flemish, but most people seem to speak some English; the television set in a corner of the LeMond living room brings in fifteen channels, including the BBC and a subscriber service from across the Channel that prints the news, including sports, in English.

"Another nice thing about Belgium, besides the English, is that you can get all these American products in the stores: root beer, Mexican taco shells, those little things that help your stay here."

Finally, LeMond said, "Belgium is centrally located. Because of all the spring races in Belgium and the Netherlands and the critériums all year round, by living here I end up spending two more months a year at home than I would by living in France."

Being at home became especially important to the LeMonds after the birth of their son, Geoffrey, in February 1984. The family lives in a quiet street with a suburban air, renting a two-story gray brick house with a small lawn in front and a big backyard with a few Corsican pines. "Those are piñon pines, imported from Nevada," LeMond joked. Another touch of home is their cocker spaniel, Brigid, like the washing machine and the dryer an American import. "We brought her back with us two years ago. European cocker spaniels aren't as gentle."

Inside, the house could belong to any American young executive. The books are by Le Carré, Forsyth, Clavell, and Ambler, with Michelin guides to Italy, Spain, Benelux, and France, in all of which LeMond has raced. Belgian scenes and framed art posters decorate the walls. There was barely a hint that the five-foot-ten-inch 150-pound LeMond is a professional bicyclist and the 1983 world champion, except for a pile of Renault jerseys next to the washing machine, some cycling magazines under the coffee table, and a small photograph on the mantel. It shows LeMond, in a business suit and tie, surrounded by an Italian youngsters' cycling team, and is inscribed in gratitude and respect for his appearance.

Like most well-known athletes, LeMond is in great demand. "Everybody wants to claim you," he said, "to invite you to dinner or to parties. We usually have to turn them down. If I did everything everybody asks me to do, my cycling would go downhill."

Offhandedly, LeMond talked about being a celebrity: "I told the neighbors we might be moving near Antwerp, mostly for the bilingual schools, English and French, when the baby begins going to school. They said, 'No, no, you can't.' It's not that I'm famous here, but a lot of people know who I am." The day he won the world championship the town planted four flagpoles in his front lawn, running up the flags of Kortrijk, Flanders, Belgium, and the United States. "Somebody stole the American flag after a few days, but the others were really knotted at the top." The city, he said, removed the poles and remaining flags a month later.

Municipal pride may be fleeting, but LeMond is not forgotten by the townspeople. He is often waved at by total strangers while riding along the Kortrijk canal on the way to his daily training run when at home. "It takes two or three minutes to get out of town on a bike. You can never get into the country in Belgium because it's all villages, but I head toward the hilly section of Flanders. I try to stay out for four or five hours a day, about a hundred and twenty or a hundred and fifty kilometers.

"When you come back, you want to relax. I just sit down on the couch and crash out, take a nap. Even mowing the lawn is quite a bit to do when you're racing. I bought a lawnmower, but we've hired a guy.

"If I raced a lot, I might be in better form physically, but you've got to be mentally strong. A lot of it is mental. But if you take a week off before an important race, you're in trouble."

LeMond almost had to take some time off after a spill late in the spring of 1984 in a race in the Netherlands. Rushed to a hospital, he was placed in intensive care for a day after a doctor diagnosed brain damage—LeMond made a face at the words—but was then released. "The doctors wanted me to stay out of riding for ten days, but that meant no Dauphiné Libéré, which meant no Tour de France." Three days later, he was competing in the Dauphiné Libéré, finishing third by winning the final time trial after a week-long and wintry ordeal through the mountains. He is both a strong climber and a time-trial specialist, two distinctions he agrees with Hinault are the keys to victory in any long race, such as the three-week Tour de France.

The Tour occupied his thoughts, and he kept a map of the course close by his seat on the couch. "It will be a very difficult Tour," he said, "very mountainous, but if I'm one hundred percent and feel good, if this didn't suit me, what would?"

Riding for Renault, he would share leadership responsibilities with Laurent Fignon, who won the Tour in 1983, just before his twenty-third birthday. "You can always use two leaders, at least for the first week," LeMond explained. "Then we'll see who's in the best position. I know I would work for him, and I think he would work for me." LeMond left no doubts that he would miss Hinault, whom he regards with respect and devotion. "We're friends," he says often and proudly. The six-year age gap seems to put them into different generations; about Fignon, a year his senior, LeMond is less warm.

Fignon said publicly over the winter that he thought LeMond would eventually leave the Renault team to make more money, an allusion to LeMond's reputation as a clever businessman—European shorthand for an American. LeMond seemed surprised by the prediction. "The only way I'd leave Renault," he said, "would be for a big American team, if a really big American team came to Europe and if I was near the end of my career."

But, he admitted, there were some drawbacks to riding for a European team. "All we ever talk about on the Renault team is bike racing. If we had another American rider, you could talk about other things: movies, other sports, investments—stuff to get you homesick." By home, he meant not Kortrijk but America.

○

When Bernard Hinault was forced to withdraw from the 1983 Tour, Renault was left with nobody resembling a leader. This might have disrupted other teams, but, aside from a few veterans, Renault without Hinault was a collection of young, zesty riders, some of them eager to see what they could do individually, and the withdrawal liberated them from all duties and devotions except to themselves. Nobody appreciated this more, or took better advantage of it, than Laurent Fignon.

Then approaching his twenty-third birthday and riding in his first Tour de France, Fignon had served Hinault as a valorous lieutenant in the Tour of Italy in 1982 and the Tour of Spain in 1983 but had not done much personally. He broke in well enough as a neophyte professional in 1982, winning the Critérium International, a prestigious spring race on the Côte d'Azur, but his first year was remembered mainly because of a mechanical accident. Riding in the Blois-Chaville race that fall, Fignon was on a breakaway, not 20 kilometers from the finish and seemingly certain of victory, when the shaft on a pedal broke, unbalancing him at full speed. He fell, of course, and the photograph of him sitting in the road, looking bewildered, with his bicycle lying behind him, was voted the best sports picture of the year.

Fignon began to realize his value the next year in the Tour of Spain, or Vuelta. He was setting the pace on a steep climb when Hinault shouted to him to slow down, that he could not keep up. The incident was forgotten as Hinault went on to win the Vuelta and Fignon finished seventh, but he had gotten the first hint of his ascendancy and Hinault's decline. "That's where I realized that I really had the stuff for stage races," Fignon said later of that Vuelta. "I recuperated well, I ate well, I slept well. I felt just fine. So there were no physical problems. Psychologically, I said to myself that I could think a little better of my chances."

Two months later, when the Tour de France started, Fignon was overlooked in all the predictions of a winner. For want of anybody better, the Renault team designated him and Marc Madiot as leaders. It was generally assumed that Renault was just along for the ride, a view that Madiot shared. "Without Hinault, we didn't expect much of ourselves, nothing more than to have somebody on the team in the first fifteen finishers, maybe Fignon or me to win a stage or two, just to show that we were around." Fignon had a grander vision. "My goal was to get to Paris wearing the white jersey of the best first-year rider in the Tour, and maybe to wear the yellow jersey a day or two."

He was thirteenth overall until the Pyrenees, when he chose the right man to follow, Pascal Simon, and went by a lot of riders still waiting for the moment to move. It was then. Fignon finished seventh on the day and moved into second place overall behind Simon, 4 minutes 22 seconds back. The next day Simon fell and broke his left shoulder blade; a week later he quit, and Fignon took over the leader's yellow jersey. He held it five more days, doing just well enough as his challengers eliminated one another, and was becoming a victor by default. Then, on the next to last stage, Fignon startled the pack by winning an individual time trial, his weakest discipline. "I got sick and tired of hearing everybody say that a Tour de France winner who doesn't win even one stage isn't a real champion," Fignon said. "So I wanted to show people something."

Afterward, when everybody was fussing over him, the blue-eyed blond-haired young cyclist established a reputation for modesty and sweetness. "The yellow jersey did things for me," he said. "Everything I did in the mountains wouldn't have been possible without the jersey. Everybody was astonished by my performance in the mountains. Well, so was I." Or, "With a dream at the end of the road, it's possible to do some surprising things."

Probably he meant these guileless statements, but there is another, deeper side to Fignon. He is a rare sort of rider, middle class and educated, even having gone briefly to a provincial college, where he studied veterinary science. This, and his wearing of glasses, which few professional riders use, was enough to get him regarded as an intellectual, a charge he is bright enough to deny. " 'Intellectual' is a pretty big word. I've been to school, but intellectual, that's a label, just a label. On a bicycle there are no academic degrees, there are just racers—good ones and less good ones."

Fignon is one of the good ones. "We don't really know his true limits," Guimard has said. "He doesn't either." Merckx had his word of praise: "Fignon inspires confidence, a pretty rider, obviously at ease." So did Anquetil: "His coolness and mastery astonished me. He's still got some things to learn about tactics, but with his punch he's going to become a super-champion."

Punch is what Fignon cares about. "I was only a middling amateur," he said, "and there certainly were classier riders. But did they have a fighting spirit? That's not so sure. That's my strength." About tactics he could be flip, saying, "There's nothing hard about it: your teammates do the work during most of the stage, and then the leader arrives to finish it off." By this time he was beginning to cash in on his Tour victory. He rode in thirty critériums and, after letting it be known that an Italian team was interested in him, negotiated a new two-year contract with Renault that nearly doubled his salary, to 18,000 francs a month. "I don't want to shock anybody," he said, "but I really do race for money. A big victory means money."

It also means a walloping taste of the good life, invitations to celebrity ski resorts, disco parties, and personal appearances at whatever chic cocktail party needs a champion bicycle rider. Flattered and fawned over and just turned twenty-three, Fignon began to believe all the wonderful things people were telling him. "I got a little carried away," he admitted months afterward. "I got a little brusque with fans and reporters. Then I remembered a warning from Gerrie Knetemann, something the Dutch rider said to me while we were on vacation on Guadeloupe: 'When you become world champion—and I have been—you can get a swelled head, but it gets deflated pretty quickly.'

"I'll be honest," Fignon added, "it happened to me. But that's over with."

As he always does, Fignon learned. "Now I understand why Hinault could sometimes be so testy," he said. "It's not so easy to separate the people who want to help you from those who don't. There's always somebody who's ready to exploit your name to make a little money for himself."

His relations with Hinault, polite when they both rode for Renault, became less so after Hinault left. "We have good relations, but they're between competitors," Fignon said, and then let slip a hint of his resentment. "Bernard won everything, and when you said something to him, he answered, 'You haven't won four Tours de France, you haven't won this, you haven't won that.' Personally I don't tell people who ask me things, 'First win the Tour de France and then we'll talk.' "

He was also critical of Merckx, mainly because Merckx became critical of him, saying, "For me, Fignon is a playboy, nothing more. You don't prepare for a race by staying out dancing until four o'clock in the morning." Fignon had a quick answer: "He gets on my nerves with all his talk about how much better and harder it was in his time. All he does is speak badly about today's riders. When I was suffering from sinusitis at the start of the season, he accused me of not doing my job. Let's not talk about Merckx."

By then Fignon was in Italy for the Giro, hoping to compensate for the bad spring he had in 1984. Sinusitis set back his training, especially during the cold and wet weather, conditions Fignon detests. He had a splendid Tour of Italy, finishing second to Francesco Moser only because the race was stolen from him. Moser, who set a record earlier in the year in Mexico for the hour's race against the clock, was a hero in Italy, and all he needed to conclude his brilliant year, even in May, was the victory that had eluded him in ten previous Giros. He got it with the help of the Italian organizers. Because of snow, they canceled the highest mountain stage, where Moser was certain to crack; they overlooked numerous pushes up hills by Moser fans and relatives and, in addition, prevented Guimard's car from approaching Fignon with advice. ("We don't ride in Italy to win," said Moreno Argentin, the 1983 Italian champion, "but to make somebody else lose.") With all this, it was discovered that Fignon suffered from a condition called hypoglycemia, which resulted in a quick discharge of adrenaline that burned up his body sugar and produced a sudden weakness. Still, Fignon held the lead into the final day, a time trial; but Moser used the aerodynamic bicycle he took with him to Mexico City to break the record for the hour and picked up nearly four minutes, to win by a little over a minute.

Finishing second, Fignon showed not Hinault's defiance but a studied acceptance. Asked if the pressure of defending his 1983 victory in the Tour de France might make him crack in the 1984 race, he responded, "No way, not after what happened in the Giro. I'm armorplated now."

And so he was, alas. The Sunday before the 1984 Tour de France he rode in the French national championships and followed the pace of a teammate, Pascal Poisson. Near the end, with Poisson struggling, Fignon easily pulled away and won. What shocked many spectators was that when he passed Poisson, Fignon neither looked at him nor made any show of sympathy. A wave of the hand, a pat on the shoulder, a smile, a shouted word—there was more than enough time for any of these, but Fignon simply rode by.

○

After a couple of days of medical examinations, publicity appearances, and training runs, the riders seemed pleased to be at last starting the Tour de France, which began with a prologue, an individual time trial, from the city hall of Montreuil. Once the town of Montreuil-sous-Bois, or Montreuil Under the Woods, it truthfully docked its name once its farms disappeared; the only reminder of its bucolic past now is a statue of a vigorous-looking peasant labeled Agriculture—the twin of one labeled Industry—at the entrance to the city hall.

The course was a short one, as prologues are, running from Montreuil to Noisy-le-Sec through streets packed with people behind barricades. A few spectators had slipped through and were badgering the racers for autographs, turning page after page of scrapbooks filled with the photographs that professional teams distribute at bicycle trade shows. Flattered, the riders almost always complied.

It is often said that bicycle racers are interested only in riding, eating, and sleeping, but on this first day they spent a fair amount of time socializing in the cultural center that served as their meeting point. Waiting for their turn to set off at one-minute intervals in the time trial, the 170 riders had a chance to greet old friends, those not seen since earlier in the season, or even since the last Tour de France. The turnover had been high during the winter, and of the seventeen teams, just Reynolds, a Spanish team, had the same ten men who rode the Tour the year before. From Spain also came the Teka team, and from Portugal, Sporting Lisbon. Italy had one representative, Carrera-Inoxpran; the Netherlands two, Panasonic and Kwantum; Switzerland one, Cilo-Aufina; Belgium two, Splendor and Europ Décor, and Columbia one, its national team, the only amateurs in the tour. France had supplied the largest delegation, seven teams: Renault, La Vie Claire, Peugeot, Skil, Coop, Système U and La Redoute. As the sociologist Richard Holt observed in *Sport and Society in Modern France,* "To a country obsessed with a fear of demographic decline, economic failure and military defeat, the Tour de France offered a comforting image of Frenchmen as tenacious, strong and swift."

The afternoon passed smoothly, with only LeMond showing any first-time jitters. Waylaid by the American television crews that continued to stalk and film him during the next three weeks, he arrived late at the starting ramp. As the big clock clicked off the seconds and the starter counted down 5-4-3-2-1, LeMond was still attaching his toe clips. In his haste, he even seemed to have forgotten to sign in officially, an infraction that costs 75 francs.

Life can be difficult in a rider's first Tour, as Modesto Urrutibeazcoa could have told LeMond.

In 1982 Urrutibeazcoa had an appointment with a few hundred of his neighbors when the race reached the Pyrenees. For the trip to Pau, in southwest France, from the Spanish village of Tolosa, the neighbors were traveling by bus. Urrutibeazcoa planned to arrive by bicycle, wearing No. 119.

"First they had three buses, but then they called to say there would be two more," he reported at the start in Basel. The agricultural village of Tolosa, near San Sebastián in the Basque country, had only 3,000 residents, so Urrutibeazcoa was obviously pleased by the promise of a big turnout. In his first Tour de France, Urrutibeazcoa, then twenty-two years old, was just beginning to realize how difficult it would be for him to attend the reunion. Of the 170 riders listed for the 1982 start, perhaps 40 were making their first appearance in the race. Only a handful were also making their debuts that year as professional riders, as the Spaniard was, but he was typical of young riders in their first Tour. Some handle it badly. Jean-Marie Grézet, then the great hope of Swiss cycling, quietly went home just before the start in 1982, saying only that he was not sure he was up to his first Tour de France.

Urrutibeazcoa tried hard to remain calm, but he admitted that there was so much to learn, especially after the second day, when he finished 133rd, more than five minutes behind the winner. "I had a puncture ten kilometers from the finish and lost more than a minute replacing the wheel," he explained, not discussing the rest of his deficit. "Anyway, it's not how you start but how you finish," he said, delivering the cliché in cheerful Spanish.

In fact, he started terribly. First, he was one of five riders, four of them Tour neophytes, who forgot to sign in before the prologue. Then, just as he rolled down the starting ramp, the chain on his bicycle rattled loose. "It was a new chain, just put on for the race. I lost twenty seconds, maybe more, catching my rhythm." His problems did not overly bother his Teka team, which did not expect much of Urrutibeazcoa; in the six months since he had turned professional, he had registered just one victory, in a stage of the Valles Mineros race in the Spanish region of Asturias. As an amateur he won ten races the year before he turned professional, including a six-day track race in Madrid, a record strong enough to get him a professional berth in the weakened world of Spanish cycling. He began racing at age fourteen, encouraged by a former professional who ran a bicycle shop in his village. Urrutibeazcoa's parents raise fruits and vegetables on their farm, and, he said, he would probably be working with them if he had not become a bicycle rider. He was very happy, he said, to be in the Tour de France. "Since I was a boy," he said, "it was always my hope to do the Tour. Now I am here, and all I want is to finish the race. The important thing is to finish." He didn't, but he did make it to Pau to meet his neighbors from Tolosa. A few days later, exhausted, he dropped out.

He did not compete in the 1983 Tour, and by 1984 had become a specialist in six-day races; he was competing in one in South America when Teka recalled him, because of an injury on its ten-man team, for the Tour, and sent him hurriedly off to France.

To the villagers of Tolosa, Urrutibeazcoa is somebody who has made it out into the great world, and they are proud of him. Once again he had an appointment with his neighbors just before the Pyrenees, he said cheerfully as he made the rounds, crying happily *"Hola,"* shaking hands, and renewing friendships.

Off to one side, Bernard Hinault was also relaxed and greeting friends. He is a specialist at Tour prologues and the intense energy they demand, having won those in Frankfurt, Basel, and Nice; he knows how to ration his strength. Not until he pushed his bicycle onto the starting ramp did he tuck down his head and begin to concentrate. "Bernard has nothing to prove in the Tour," said his teammate Alain Vigneron, "but he can win the esteem of the public and gain a true and great popularity." This was a fair analysis, but did Hinault share it? He had long said that a fifth victory, which would tie him with Eddy Merckx and Jacques Anquetil, meant nothing to him as a record, that victories, not records, interested him. How important to him was the esteem of the public, which he had not bothered to seek—or even pretended to seek—for years?

What seemed more likely was that even after his spring races and the tests in the mountains of the Dauphiné Libéré, he was still worried about his knee. And, of course, he wanted revenge. The French say that revenge is a dish best eaten cold, but as he drew his body tighter on his bicycle seat and finally lifted his head to stare down the course, Hinault was tight with passion.

Anquetil said the next day that had he been riding in his first stage of the Tour de France in two years, he would not have gone all out for victory, that he would not have shown his opponents so early in the race in something as meaningless as the prologue that he was in top condition. This made sense tactically but not emotionally. Rejected by Renault, chivied all spring by questions about his health, written off by so many people as too old, Hinault had no time for prudence. The Badger had come home to the Tour de France.

For a while at the finish in Noisy-le-Sec, Alan Peiper of the Peugeot team was ranked first in the time trial in 6 minutes 48 seconds. "It's not over yet," he cautioned. "There are three or four good riders still to come."

Soon Hinault arrived, surprising really no one by finishing in the best time, 6 minutes 39 seconds. Spent, he was led by Philippe Crépel, his team manager, to the special mobile home La Vie Claire had outfitted as a press center. Hinault spread himself over two armchairs and was told by an onlooker, "You did well, really well." Another witness said, "I've never seen such a glow of happiness in his eyes."

Wearing an aerodynamic helmet and the leader's yellow jersey, carried over from the previous Tour, Fignon was the last to start. He knew Hinault's time and came close to beating it before he finished in 6 minutes 42 seconds, good enough for second place. "Everybody wants to make this Tour a duel between Hinault and Fignon," Crépel commented, "and they're right. Today we see the first result."

Later Hinault remarked, "It's funny, but I feel like nothing's changed." At that point the yellow jersey had been returned to him for the first time since July 25, 1982, when he stood on the victory podium on the Champs-Elysées and looked down into the faces of a sea of believers.

○

Another Tour de France, the first for women, began the day after the men's prologue, and Mieke Havik of the Netherlands earned herself a footnote in bicycling history by winning the sprint finish of the opening stage.

"That's something, to be the first winner," said Marianne Martin of the American team in admiration. She finished third, consoled by the fact that there was a women's race and that she was part of it. "You only get one chance to be in the first Tour de France," she said happily. A Canadian rider, Senta Bauermeister, agreed: "It's really historic just being here."

This sense of history was strong in the field of thirty-six women divided into six teams representing five countries. France entered two teams, and the United States, Canada, the Netherlands, and Britain one each.

The women's course was modeled on the men's, covering part of the same daily stages, roughly the final third over which the men raced. International bicycling rules limit women amateurs—there are no professionals—to racing 80 kilometers a day. In all, the women were to ride 991 kilometers, an average of 55 a day, while the men were to cover 4,019 kilometers. Although the general course was to be the same, the women were excused from climbing the highest mountains, getting instead five days off to the men's one. They were also competing for much smaller prizes, a total of 100,000 francs, compared with twenty-five times that for the men.

The leader of the American team was expected to be Betsy King, a thirty-two-year-old rider, but in a training run earlier that week she had cut her left knee badly, and her doctor considered it doubtful that she could ride in the women's Tour de France. She entered anyway, heavily bandaged from mid-thigh to mid-calf. "It's bad, but I wasn't about to miss this," she said.

She showed the same spirit earlier in the spring, when she started the Bordeaux-Paris race two hours before everybody else and finished last, more than an hour after the winner—a result that was unanimously considered a great triumph.

"I'm doing this to say, Hey, man, we count, too. Women are important," King explained before the 586-kilometer Bordeaux-Paris race, the world's longest one-day race and France's oldest, begun in 1891 and run in 1984 for the eighty-first time. Never before had a woman entered.

"I look forward to this as much as you look forward to getting your wisdom teeth out," King had said in Bordeaux, "but it has to be done. A lot of people think women can't ride a race like this, so somebody's got to do it to show them a woman won't die."

Although she was far behind when the field finished at Fontenay-sous-Bois, an eastern suburb of Paris, few of the thousands of spectators left before her arrival, some 18 hours after she set out. A wave of applause swept up the final hill with King as she followed a pace-setting motorbike, trying hard, and utterly failing, to conceal her satisfaction with the cries of "Bravo, Betsy."

Most races do not specifically exclude women, but classic professional races are rarely open to amateurs. Bordeaux-Paris is an exception, allowing licensed professionals and amateurs. That was the opening for King, a native of Farmington, Connecticut, who had been riding as an amateur for French clubs since 1981 but had never thought of entering a men's professional race. "I am above all a woman, but I am not above all a feminist," she said.

Yet she had chafed against the French and International Cycling Union rules that limit women's competition: no more than one race a day, that race not to exceed 80 kilometers, no competition against men except on Sundays and holidays, and such competition not to exceed 120 kilometers.

She was also disturbed by what she described as men's unwillingness to lose to a woman. "I win races with ninety people in them every Sunday, but the people are all women," she said. "When I race against men, they'll block the course and help each other just to stop me. I know I can win against men. I'm really nasty when I'm riding, and the Lord gave me a good body. I have a lot of power." She pulled up the left leg of her Renault team sweatpants and showed her calf. "That's muscle, more muscle than a woman is supposed to have," she said. Standing 5 feet 3 inches, she weighs 115 pounds.

When Gérard Labarthe, the trainer for her club at Antony-Bercy, outside Paris, suggested that she enter Bordeaux-Paris, King was ready if not quite willing. Her intention to compete, which caused some growls, was made public during the winter while she was visiting her parents in Connecticut. After that visit she tried to make the U.S. team for the Olympic Games, and then returned to France in the spring. When she learned that she would be allowed to race in Bordeaux-Paris, she recalled, "I couldn't back out. All I could think was, Here I go off to the sacrifice."

She competed not as an official entry but in an unspecified and singular category, starting alone two hours before the men. She was caught and passed by all of them late the next afternoon, but the point was that she finished and showed that a woman had the strength and stamina to participate in such a long race.

As King rode, she was loudly cheered. "It was like all of France was pushing me," she said. "There were lots of people yelling, 'Allez, Betsy.' This, and finishing, meant a lot.

"Suddenly a lot of women riders are saying to me, 'I didn't know we could do Bordeaux-Paris. Next year I'll ride it too.' I've made my point."

She had, but not totally. Asked about his feelings regarding the women's Tour de France, Jacques Anquetil said in his newspaper column: "I have absolutely nothing against women's sports, but I find that cycling is far too difficult for a woman. They're not made for the sport.

"I prefer to see women in a short white skirt rather than racing shorts. In fact, I like women a lot and am really sorry to see them suffer. On a bicycle, there's always a lot of suffering."

Hearing about this, most of the riders in the first women's Tour de France merely rolled their eyes.

FOUR

When *the race finally broke free of Seine-*Saint-Denis, it was Sunday, and so everybody went for a ride in the country, as the French do on Sunday. The day's stage, the Tour's second, was to cover 249 kilometers northeast to Louvroil in the start of a two-day penetration of what is now the Nord Department, the North, formerly Flanders. For about the first 20 kilometers the road passed through anonymous suburbs until the fields on either side turned green and brown, no longer filled with gray stone houses in need of upkeep.

The crowds were larger than might have been expected of such sparse country, but it was Sunday and the first day of July besides, the start of the four-week French vacation, which, despite folklore, not all the French take in August. That alone could not explain the crowds, since the Tour was heading north and the French swarm south on vacation, accompanied by Belgians, Dutch, Danes, Swedes, and Germans yearning for sun and heat. But there they stood, lining each turn and rise, many of the men in cycling jerseys. Bicycling is practiced on a club level throughout France, with riders passing up the ranks based on age until they catch the eye of a top-flight amateur team, many of them affiliated with a professional team. At age twenty, a rider may turn professional, but if he is any good, he will long since have signed a letter of intent with a professional team. If he does not attract one, he can continue to race with the amateurs until he begins to feel uncomfortable competing against boys or, worse, losing to them. Then he decides he is not breaking training if he has a few beers with his friends, because he is no longer really in training. At lunch with the gang from his factory or garage, he will eat sandwiches or French fries, and soon he is barely able to squeeze into his racing jersey. Luckily it is sold in an extra-large size in most cycling shops. By the time he is thirty, the rider who was a great hope in his local cycling club when he was seventeen is now the man at the side of the road in black shorts and striped jersey as the Tour comes by. The professionals carry fruit in the pockets of their jersey, but he will have stuffed his with a chunk of sausage, a piece of cheese, and some bread, and his water bottle is filled with red wine. While the race passes, he and his buddies, similarly dressed and leaning on their bicycles, compliment this rider's style or criticize that rider's bearing. Afterward they lay their bicycles in the grass and enjoy their picnic; it is, after all, a Sunday in the country.

The Tour itself was only slightly more animated. The day before, Franck Hoste of the Europ Décor team had won the sprint finish of the first stage and picked up enough bonus seconds—actually a deduction from his overall time—touring the Seine-Saint-Denis towns to take the yellow jersey from Bernard Hinault, who was less than a minute behind.

Hinault would have ample opportunity to regain the 30 seconds Hoste had won by finishing first. Two types of time bonuses were available: reductions of up to 30 seconds from the times of the first three finishers of each stage, plus up to 12 minus seconds for the first three at specified bonus sprints, or "hot spots," along the way. Besides time reductions and financial prizes, points were awarded at—ranging up to 35 on the flat and 12 in the mountains—to determine the wearer of the green jersey, the points leader.

Nothing stirred until the first bonus sprint, when Eddy Planckaert, a sprint specialist with the Panasonic team, found himself dueling with Greg LeMond, the world champion, for a 12-second bonus. Planckaert should have won but did not, overcome with amazement, like somebody at a country auction suddenly realizing that the other bidder for an old brass bed is the Getty Museum.

The day passed quietly, hot but not oppressively so because of a head wind that was strong enough to cool down the passion for breakaways. "Everybody watched everybody else," LeMond later explained. "There was no chance of an exploit." There was also no daily prize for combativeness. Every once in a while somebody made a desultory attempt to escape, but it was obvious that he didn't mean it, and the pack turned up its pace a hair and quickly brought him back. Strategy dictated a breakaway attempt by one of the weaker teams, those that had no strong mountain climber, because the first ten days were all the race they had. But the road was narrow, allowing no more than three men abreast, and they blocked escape. For now the riders seemed most concerned with staying out of one another's way in such a big field, avoiding the accidental grazing of wheels that can cause a crash. Still it happened: at kilometer 78, a tight left-hand turn through the village of Faverolles, Jean-René Bernaudeau of the Système U team fell, scraping a knee. Everybody managed to ride around him.

Sunday in the country. Dumas *père* grew up near Faverolles, and it was there that Victor Hugo had Jean Valjean steal the loaf of bread in *Les Misérables.* Asked for a cheese sandwich, the owner of a small café in Neufchelles proudly produced a cheese board with five or six varieties, and invited his customer to make his own sandwich. Near Condé-sur-Aisne, a young pheasant flapped across the road. Potatoes, it seems, do not simply grow like lumps of coal in the earth but put out a large and delicate green leaf. The rolling fields were broken by thickets of trees in which who knows how many soldiers died in World War I. At kilometer 198, Giovanni Battaglin of the Carrera-Inoxpran team, Claude Criquielion of Splendor, and Edgar Corredor of Teka all fell and quickly remounted. The crowds were especially large in Laon, where the road leading up to the ancient fortress was jammed. Some spectators carried signs for Hinault and some for Fignon; one boy stood on his lawn with a hand-lettered sign that said, *"Que le meilleur gagne"*—may the best man win.

This is farming country, not so rich as in the Loire Valley but still fertile enough to impress an Irish visitor, who marveled that so much of the land could be given over to grain. For miles on the right the fields are planted in wheat and barley; on the left they are planted in potatoes.

Sunday in the country. The pack was still under control. Near Crécy-sur-Serre, across a field patchworked with brown barley and dark green kale, the riders descended a hill in what looked, from a distance, like slow motion. A multicolored column of ants was on the move. The sun was still hot, the head wind cool.

The fields gave out long before Louvroil, where the race was eagerly awaited. As a local newspaper put it: "What a pretty picture the Tour de France made sweeping into Louvroil, through the heart of red and gray houses, those houses of the North that go so well with bicycling. Through the heart, also, of an enormous crowd, excited and vibrant. Louvroil, a workers' city, a city stunned like its neighbors in the Sambre Basin by its industrial difficulties, Louvroil became suddenly the most-watched city in Europe. By the magic of a pack of cyclists, by the magic of the Tour de France. From now on no sports-minded Belgian, Dutchman, German, Swiss, Spaniard, Italian, or even Colombian will no longer not know of our existence. They'll also know that hidden in this place are treasures of dynamism that allowed a welcome with flawless efficiency for the greatest cycling race in the world."

As the riders passed the finish line for the first time and began a 5-kilometer circuit, they were still bunched. With half a kilometer to go, Marc Madiot of the Renault team fought clear and finished first by 2 seconds. The yellow jersey was taken over by Jacques Hanegraaf of the Kwantum team because of bonus time won en route.

The medical bulletin said Bernaudeau and Philippe Leleu of the Vie Claire team had been treated for skinned left knees, Francis Castaing of Peugeot for conjunctivitis, Corredor for a bruised left shoulder, Marc Sergeant of Europ Décor for an injured left thumb, and Alfonso Florez of the Colombian team for a superficial scalp cut and scraped left knee and elbow after a fall. Florez was streaming blood down his face when he finished and looked a sight, but was chipper the next morning.

Jaime Vilamajo of the Reynolds team was fined 75 francs and penalized 10 seconds for receiving a bag of food from his team manager at kilometer 158, or 16 kilometers beyond the feeding zone, where the riders whiz through and grab a *musette,* a light sack of food. His manager was fined 375 francs. Claude Vincendeau of the Système U team was fined 50 francs for stopping on the left side of the road, instead of the regulation right, after he had a flat. His manager was fined 100 francs for replacing the tire while his rider was on the wrong side of the road.

The crowd continued celebrating in Louvroil for some hours after the riders left for their hotels. For them, the race would continue tomorrow, and Sunday in the country was over.

○

Professional bicycling, some of the more independent riders like to say, is an individual sport practiced in teams. This can be true enough, but not in the Tour's sole team time trial, when, in the name of aerodynamics, each individual must subordinate himself to the team effort.

The rules are simple: Setting off four minutes apart, each team races against the clock. The rules specify that the time when a team's fifth man crosses the finish line is given to all the first five, with the second five getting their actual individual times. A penalty system costs each team behind the winner a graduated amount of time, down to 2 minutes 30 seconds for the last-place team.

For the 40 to 60 kilometers of the time trial, teams ride in as tight a formation as the ten men can form. Often for no more than a minute or two, the man in front sets the fastest pace he can, then slips back and the next man takes his turn at the front. This relates to the law of aerodynamics that says that by relaying each other, two men can ride faster longer than one man can do alone and that three men can do better than two, four men better than three, and so on up to about ten or twelve men, when another law, that of diminishing returns, begins to apply. Until then, the followers benefit from the prowlike effect of the leader as he blocks the wind and slices through the air barrier, which, even on a still day, provides resistance. As he moves, the leader creates a slipstream in which his partner rides with perhaps half the effort required of the man in front, the respite of relaying.

On a typical day, the pack moves at about 40 kilometers an hour, but this speed is far below the record in the team time trial, which was added to the Tour de France in 1978. Since then, the best time, over 40 kilometers in 1981, was just under 52 kilometers an hour. This was set by the Raleigh team, which had the motors, as time-trial specialists may be called, men who can set a pace for 4 or 5 minutes, drop back for a breather, and then come to the front again. Sponsored for many years by the British bicycle manufacturers and based in the Netherlands, Raleigh found a new primary sponsor during the winter, Panasonic, the Japanese electronics company. With Panasonic's new money, the team manager, Peter Post, dropped some veterans and rebuilt the formation, sacrificing the motors for sprinters. Some of his former riders joined a new Dutch team, Kwantum, and feuded with Panasonic-Raleigh for the headlines at home. Thus far in the Tour, Kwantum had a monopoly, with one of its riders wearing the yellow jersey for the start of the 51-kilometer race.

So in the Tour's third stage Panasonic was looking for a victory in what had been its specialty. Enrolling so many of the old Raleigh motors, Kwantum was also hopeful. Many other teams had a reason to want to do well in the time trial. La Vie Claire needed a good showing since it obviously would not be of much help to Bernard Hinault in the mountains, and this was its main chance to contribute to its leader. Coop, which had no strong leader or climber, was motivated because it was the defending champion in the team time trial. Another French team, La Redoute, sponsored by a mail-order company based in nearby Roubaix, was eager for publicity in its corporate backyard. The Belgians were also close to home and their public, but none of their teams were considered to be strong enough to trouble the favorites—Panasonic, Kwantum, and Renault.

The three differed in tactics. At Kwantum, cyclist Ludo Peeters explained, "We use the Raleigh method, since so many of us know it. It's a machine to swallow the kilometers. The road captain gives the orders, and the man in front stays there as long as he can." At Panasonic, the Raleigh method had been discarded after the loss of the motors. "It's not the man in front who sets the pace but the second man, who forces the pace by trying to take the lead," a team official said. "That's where you get your dynamism." At Renault, Cyrille Guimard, the team manager, had a third method. "We don't have a designated road captain. Everybody listens to everybody else. The strongest will provide the speed, and we'll use long relays."

Another question with different answers was what to do when a rider had a flat. This depended on who and where and which team. Sometimes a team waited for a needed rider, as Skil did when Gilles Mas punctured. Because Mas was a climber and would be needed in the weeks ahead, and because Skil could be an uncommonly cohesive team, it dropped its pace while the team mechanic replaced his wheel. (As old photographs show, riders used to carry a spare tire strapped to their backs, but it took them up to 3 minutes to replace the tire and a mechanic can do it in 30 seconds, so nobody wears a tire any longer.) When Skil raced as the Sem team in 1983, it also waited for Joaquim Agostinho, who skidded and fell just after the start. If he had fallen 5 kilometers farther along, the team might not have waited, since there would have been that much less distance in which to make up the 30 seconds. Half a minute over 51 kilometers may not seem like much time, but it is often the difference between winning and placing fifth or seventh.

Panasonic knew this and left behind, or dropped, Bert Oosterbosch when he punctured 15 kilometers after the start and fell. The decision was surprising, since Oosterbosch had won two individual time trials in 1983 and was one of the few Raleigh motors left with Panasonic. "Oosterbosch would have made a big difference to the team for the first ten days, but he was having a bad day, very heavy in the legs, and when he punctured, we left him," Post explained. For a single rider without benefit of relays, there was no catching up to the train ahead. Oosterbosch finished 13 minutes behind his team and, nearly in tears, was told that he had been eliminated from the Tour de France on time differential.

This rule, using a complex mathematical formula based on the winner's time, is rarely invoked en masse, even in the mountains, where a horde of riders can straggle in beyond the limit. But in a time trial it is used as a goad to force riders to keep up. Disqualification on time differential is a humiliating but honorable way to go, unlike such other grounds for dismissal as repeated infractions of the rules of conduct or drug fraud.

Another team, Système U, made a similar decision to drop a rider, when Claude Vincendeau punctured at kilometer 6. He too was eliminated on time differential, setting off public criticism of their manager by some riders. The dispute was magnified because Vincendeau was the son of a high official in Système U, a chain of supermarkets in its first year of sponsorship. Many of the team's riders, who raced in 1983 for the Wolber team and were left stranded when it dropped its sponsorship, seemed to fear the effect that Vincendeau's disqualification would have on the boss. The team manager, Marcel Boishardy, did nothing to help. "We're all guilty," he admitted. "I didn't stop them, they didn't wait. Everybody was wrong."

The road from Louvroil to Valenciennes was somewhat hilly and roughly straight until about 10 kilometers from the finish, where it turned right. The wind was frontal for the time trial and at the right turn became a side wind, the kind that pushes riders along. Going off first in inverse order of ranking, as the rules specify for time trials, the Colombians were a hapless sight in a discipline unknown in their country, where individuality is emphasized. They started in a ragged formation and never did manage to get together. "We fell apart in the last fifty kilometers," Alfonso Lopez tried to joke about the 51-kilometer race. Later a familiar question was revived: Were the Colombians afraid of pain? The team time trial tests riders' ability to bear pain, to pedal as rapidly and strongly as possible for about an hour. There is rarely time to shift position and relieve the strain on shoulders and back. One quality that makes a rider faster than another is the ability to bear pain, or knowing how to suffer, as the riders put it.

"What makes a champion is mostly character, pride, and the ability to suffer," Ferdinand Julien explained after finishing his fourth Tour de France in the late 1970s. "There's always a moment, going up a mountain, where the best man is the one who knows how to suffer."

The team time trial offered few consolations for the pain, but there was one that appealed to some riders: by pushing themselves as hard as they could, they inflicted the same torture on their teammates, a factor not to be disregarded on a factionalized team.

At kilometer 30, Panasonic held a 7-second lead over Kwantum. In

Raleigh's golden days, it had so many motors that it could race in double file, two lines of five men tucked tight side by side. Now Panasonic was in the traditional single file and, despite its lead, in trouble with Oosterbosch gone and Peter Winnen, the team's major climber, having an off day and just hanging on at the rear. Panasonic could not afford to leave him behind.

Renault was 15 seconds behind Panasonic but not worrying, because Guimard had figured things out: "The night before we all went by car to look at the course. We realized that twelve kilometers from the finish there was a small hill followed by a gentle rise, and we decided that there was the place to attack. And that's exactly what my boys did." Renault turned up its speed and all ten riders finished together, first in 1 hour 3 minutes 54 seconds. Panasonic and Kwantum tied for second, 4 seconds behind. Despite the motivation, La Vie Claire could do no more for Hinault than finish sixth, probably better than it should have done, but not enough better to scare anybody. As expected, the Colombians were last, in 1 hour 10 minutes 14 seconds.

Guimard disparaged Renault's victory, trying to keep the team's confidence in line. "What's a four-second victory?" he asked. "A badly handled relay, a badly negotiated curve?" He was right—just that and not much more, but the warning was there: Renault did not intend to handle relays or curves badly.

○

The Tour de France had decided to give a medal to Jean Stablinski for long and devoted service to the race and, naturally enough, chose to do this in his hometown of Valenciennes—on the main square, in fact, so that nobody could doubt that the Tour had a special place in its heart for the desolate North and its sons. Glowering and bulky, they filled the square between the end of the team time trial and the start of the afternoon's stage to Béthune, the only two-stage day of the Tour. Like Stablinski, many of them were the children of miners welcomed from Poland after both world wars to dig the region's coal and pour its steel.

They were no more than polite as the medal was given to Stablinski, four times bicycling champion of France, world champion in 1962, and an indifferent team manager in the 1970s, fired by Gitane when he alienated and overworked Bernard Hinault in his first year as a professional. Since then Stablinski had become a driver for the Tour, with the plum assignment of chauffeuring commentators for one of the television channels. He liked to strut around with them at the end of the day, acting in no way like a hired hand, and was always available for a comment or bit of advice, even if nobody asked. His medal was generally considered to be less a reflection of his individual merit than an attempt by the Tour to win some hearts and minds, especially those that might be planning a protest demonstration, using a stoppage of the race to gain publicity for their cause.

Unemployed steelworkers had done this before, as had farmers and students and shipyard workers, and the Tour was making a special effort in 1984 to show its concern for the country's economic crisis, especially during this visit to the North. In addition to the traditional bouquet and kiss on the cheek from Miss France, the beauty queen, the winner of a day's stage might also find himself getting a miner's hat from the local president of a union; a truck had even been added to the publicity caravan to distribute literature calling for relief for the steel industry. Nobody could accuse the Tour of being oblivious to the real world.

So Stablinski got his medal, and photographs of the ceremony appeared in newspapers throughout the North and in Belgium too. Not 25 kilometers from the Belgian border, Valenciennes and its Slavic people are part of a France far different from the Latin lands in the south or even the sleek suburbs of Paris only 200 kilometers away. Beer is the drink here, not wine, and competing breweries have staked out many of the town's corners: Stella Artois, Kronenbourg, Porter 39, and Kanterbrau. Churches are in the Flemish style, with modified onion domes, and in front of the cathedral stands a bust of the heroic Albert I, king of the Belgians and leader of their army during World War I, with the inscription, "Sacrifices, suffering, and hopes have cemented France and Belgium." Not that they have in the rest of the country, where the Belgian joke is the French equivalent of the Polish or Irish joke, but perhaps they have here.

Once one of the innumerable "Athenses of the north" because of its museums and art schools, Valenciennes is a sad place now, overlooked in the French economic leap forward of the 1970s, when the rest of the country moved into an age of consumerism as the gross national product trebled between 1965 and 1975 and then nearly doubled again by 1980. Everything took off in that heady time: during the decade the number of French homes with telephones rose from 15 percent to 75 percent, with television sets from 70 percent to more than 90 percent, with cars from 56 percent to more than 70 percent. Students replaced their modest motorbikes with imported motorcycles. In 1970 many buildings in Paris still had communal toilets in the courtyard, and public urinals stood on streetcorners. By 1980 they were gone. Frozen foods became popular and so did lavish gifts at Christmas, until then a quiet day in a secular country. In the Paris métro, the old women who used to punch tickets were replaced by turnstiles and patrols of inspectors seeking out the multitudes who jumped over the bars. Never before a people willing to travel outside their borders, the French were now to be found spending their vacations in Spain and Scandinavia, Italy and Greece. The franc was strong, dipping under four to the dollar in the middle of the decade, and it bought not just luxuries like washing machines and toasters—no more wire racks over a gas flame —but stereo systems and color television sets.

The North was not left out, but its economy was moderated by its dependence on steel and coal, and other countries were finding cheaper ways to produce them. By 1982, a year after the Socialists came to power and nearly 150 billion francs had fled the country in fright, France realized it had to modernize its steel industry. Markets had shrunk and the European Economic Community had agreed that all governmental steel subsidies had to end by 1987. The first step was a governmental investment of 15 billion francs to increase production capacity and a cut of 12,000 jobs. The steel work force that was nearly 150,000 men in the 1970s was down to 97,000 by 1983. By the next year, the government was projecting 10,000 to 12,000 more layoffs. Nor was steel the only industry affected; shipbuilding, automobile production, and coal mining were also being streamlined. By early 1983, Socialist policies were marked by a 12 percent inflation rate, a 90-billion-franc trade deficit, and three devaluations of the franc. The government shifted course from creating jobs to controlling inflation and the trade deficit: the new policy called for lowering government spending, increasing taxes, and shifting the focus from nationalized heavy industries to high technology. The austerity program saw unemployment rise to 2.3 million people, a tenth of the work force. It was hard to tell from the stores, with video boutiques sprouting throughout Paris, but the boom was over. They knew it all along in Valenciennes, and so Stablinski got his medal.

Perhaps the gambit worked. In its few days in the North, the Tour passed many padlocked mills but had no problems with demonstrators, unlike the day in 1982 when a protest by steelworkers over the planned closing of their plant in Denain stopped the race and forced the first cancellation of a daily stage in the Tour's history.

That day the race was scheduled to end in Fontaine-au-Piré, a northern village of 1,250 inhabitants, two cafés, a school, a church, a few shops, two small textile plants, and many small farms. It would have been the most memorable day for Fontaine-au-Piré since August 15, 1793, when it was pillaged by Austrian troops, and far more joyful, since it would have been the fulfillment of a four-year effort by the town to become the smallest community ever to have welcomed a day's finish of the Tour de France.

"Nobody took us seriously," said the mayor, Jean-Marie Lemaire. His village was so small that the mayor's job was passed from father to son, and had been for generations; thus the family name, Lemaire (meaning the mayor). When he and a local delegation first went to Paris to present their bid, he recalled, "The organizers smiled. They showed me all it would take—money, equipment, all the enormous demands the Tour makes. Everybody smiled. But Fontaine-au-Piré remained a candidate." A year later the village won its case and was listed as the finishing point of the fifth stage of the 1982 Tour.

"I didn't dare announce the news immediately," Lemaire continued. "I waited until the official map was published, showing Fontaine-au-Piré. Until then, nobody would have believed me."

That fall the village began to prepare. Roads to be used by the bicyclists were resurfaced, sidewalks were repaired, a dressing room with showers was built, houses were repainted. To raise funds, the village became a gigantic factory. Cottage industries sprang up to produce T-shirts, hats, pennants, gadgets of all kinds for sale in the region. Everybody worked at night, after regular jobs, except for pensioners and schoolchildren, who worked during the day. A bank loan was arranged and a raffle, with gifts worth 15,000 francs, was set up. More than 17,000 tickets were sold.

Alerted by 50,000 brochures distributed in the North, a large crowd gathered in Fontaine-au-Piré. Flowers awaited each of the teams, and the town hall was decorated with the flag of each nation represented in the Tour de France. Champagne was on ice.

But the riders had been stopped 40 kilometers away in Denain. By the time the protesting steelworkers dispersed, the riders were gone by car to their hotels for the next day's stage. Some officials made it by car to Fontaine-au-Piré, but none of the riders did. The village was promised another chance in 1983, and this time nobody made any trouble, not even when the Tour passed through Saint-Gobain, where the glass factories had laid off workers, or through Origny-Sainte-Benoîte, where the cement works had cut back production.

It was calm all along the route, in fact, until, a year late, the Tour de France reached Fontaine-au-Piré, where the joy and excitement lasted throughout the night.

○

Northward, through more steel and coal country, through battle-grounds of World Wars I and II. Near the end of the fourth stage, an 83-kilometer run from Valenciennes to Béthune, the road signs pointed to Armentières and Dunkerque. The Dud Corner British Military Cemetery, with its sign of tribute to 17,000 men missing in action, faced the road, framed by distant slag heaps balding through their bit of grass. All along the route the crowds were vast: Where did all the people come from in Douai on a Monday afternoon? Hundreds of thousands saw the race, standing firm even when it began to rain heavily late in the day.

Many teams were looking for victory in this stage. Kwantum, delighted to be overshadowing its Dutch rival Panasonic, wanted to keep the yellow jersey another day. Panasonic needed a victory badly to win back the headlines from Kwantum. Coop, which had no strong challenger in the mountains, had less than a week left on the flat. Peugeot, a weak fourth in this morning's team time trial after victory the year before, needed to make amends. Instead it was La Redoute, the team based nearby in Roubaix and eager for some splash, that made the first move, sending Ferdi Van den Haute off and away at kilometer 25.

This was a good choice, especially since no team was yet trying to control the race by sending a man to tag along with each breakaway.

Laurent Fignon of the Renault team and a Eurovision cameraman on a motorcycle.

Greg LeMond of the Renault team at home in Belgium.

Bernard Hinault of the Vie Claire team during an individual time trial at La Ruchère en Chartreuse (sixteenth stage).

Fans examining the riders' bicycles before a daily stage.

A veteran amateur rider salutes the Tour de France.

Modesto Urrutibeazcoa of the Teka team at the start of his first Tour de France, 1982.

Before the day's stage, time to sign autographs.

Sunday in the country—the pack enters a village (second stage).

Mieke Havik of the Dutch team wins the first stage of the first Women's Tour de France.

Betsy King of the U.S. team.

The Women's Tour de France heading into the Alps.

Phil Anderson leading the Panasonic team in the team time trial (third stage).

Bert Oosterbosch of the Panasonic team falls and is left behind in the team time trial (third stage).

Vincent Barteau of the Renault team leads Paulo Ferreira of Sporting Lisbon and Maurice Le Guilloux of La Vie Claire in the three-man breakaway to Cergy-Pontoise.

Maurice Le Guilloux.

Sunday in the country (second stage).

Down go the riders in a spill.

Sean Kelly of the Skil team.

Joaquim Agostinho, who fell and rose and fell again.

Franck Hoste of the Europ Decor team (right) beats Sean Kelly of the Skil team as Gilbert Glaus of the Cilo-Aufina team raises his hand in protest to Kelly's foul (Alençon, sixth stage).

Sean Kelly (right) of the Skil team beats Laurent Fignon of the Renault team (center) and Kim Andersen of Coop at a bonus sprint.

Bernard Hinault of La Vie Claire comforts his injured teammate Christian Jourdan just before Jourdan was forced to quit the race.

Alain Meslet, once a rider, then a chauffeur.

Eric Vanderaerden of the Panasonic team demonstrating a sprinter's trick as he attempts to pass Ludo Peeters of the Kwantum team.

Robert Millar of the Peugeot team, leading Jean-René Bernaudeau of the Systeme U team and Gerard Veldscholten of Panasonic on the climb to Guzet-Neige (eleventh stage).

Joop Zoetemelk of Kwantum leading Henk Lubberding of Panasonic and Robert Millar of Peugeot in the Pyrenees.

COR VOS

Martin Ramirez of the Systeme U team (right) and Adri van der Poel of Kwantum finish the stage in a bus after quitting (fourteenth stage).

GRAHAM WATSON

Joop Zoetemelk of the Kwantum team.

COR VOS

Francisco Rodriguez of the Splendor team cooling off at the finish of a day's race with a bottle of Perrier.

Eddy Merckx, retired from racing to become a team official in the 1978 Tour.

Eric Vanderaerden of Panasonic, cooling off after a stage.

Laurent Fignon of the Renault team climbing in the Pyrenees.

Fons de Wolf of the Europ Decor team on his winning breakaway to the Domaine du Rouret (fourteenth stage).

Marianne Martin of the American team, winner of the first Women's Tour de France.

Phil Anderson of the Panasonic team (left) and Michel Laurent of the Coop team.

Laurent Fignon celebrates his victory in the time trial at La Ruchère en Chartreuse (sixteenth stage).

Greg LeMond of the Renault team in the individual time trial at La Ruchère en Chartreuse (sixteenth stage).

The riders prepare for a long day by squeezing their own orange juice.

Ad Wijnands of the Kwantum team picking up lunch on the fly.

Adri van der Poel of the Kwantum team off on a breakaway, accompanied by a team car and followed by a photographer's motorcycle.

Even so, a respected rider would be followed immediately by any of several teams, since his strength and reserves were known—and so an important rider rarely attempted a breakaway on the flat. That job was usually left to a lesser rider, like Van den Haute, who will often be allowed to seek his fortune on the assumption that he will fail. Even when he doesn't, if he starts off far down in the standings, the time he gains will not threaten the leaders. Bernard Hinault summed up the pack mentality when he said later, "The Belgian wasn't dangerous, so we let him do it." Van den Haute ranked ninety-sixth overall, already 4 minutes 30 seconds behind the yellow jersey.

For all this calculation, when a strong team is controlling the race, the breakaway can be rare. "I'm partly responsible," Jacques Anquetil has admitted. "When I was winning, I realized that this little game was dangerous because a rider could take ten minutes from you and then discover hitherto unknown gifts as a climber and become an opponent of a quality you never suspected. So with the help of my team we raised the pack's pace so high that we destroyed the chances of breakaways and long gains. Merckx didn't change that strategy either. It makes the race less spectacular but much more efficient."

Over this rigorously flat country Van den Haute took a while to get out of sight, so nobody could complain later that communications had failed, that nobody actually realized a rider had broken away. Riders are supposed to pass along information during a breakaway, and a motorcyclist with a blackboard cruises between the lead rider and the pack to show each the chalked time difference between them. But occasionally the collective memory fails. What happens then is that the second man to finish, usually the winner of the group sprint, will throw up his arms in triumph, forgetting—or never having known—that a breakaway rider arrived minutes earlier and is probably watching, amused, beyond the finish line.

Riding with a strong side wind that pushed him along, Van den Haute briskly left the pack behind. In 5 kilometers he built a lead of 1 minute 53 seconds; 10 kilometers farther along he was 6 minutes 23 seconds ahead. By the time he entered Douai, he had the city to himself as he pumped along in his ungainly way, all long legs and knees, down the gray main street. A great cheer followed him because crowds love a breakaway, which means there really is a race, with the pack chasing the solo rider. Otherwise the pack comes through as one long whoosh, a displacement of air that sends the dust blowing, and then the day is over. Riders too love breakaways and their scent of glory at the end of the road. "For prestige and publicity, there's nothing like doing well in the Tour," Van den Haute said later. "Everybody gets to know you."

In French, the language of bicycling, a breakaway is an *échappé,* an offshoot from the verb meaning to escape. Escape, get away from it all, break away: the language of travel agents. Immune to responsibility or bills or telephone calls, beyond the reach of preachy wives or unjust bosses, the breakaway is riding for every envious man watching him and cheering that the escape will never end. Van den Haute rode on, a lone eagle oblivious to the motorcycle policemen and official, press and team cars that surrounded him. Behind him the pack remained restrained, too weary or confident that he could not take the yellow jersey. At kilometer 57, these calculations went wrong and Van den Haute was 6 minutes 37 seconds ahead and the race's leader "on the road"—the riders' term for that shadow world where all things are possible because the race is not yet over. On the road, where Ferdi Van den Haute, from his crow's nest atop the highest mast, would be first to spot the brown smudge on the horizon that meant the New World and wealth unimagined.

Slowly the pack came alive and the lead began to shrink. Twelve kilometers from Béthune rain began to fall, and the side wind that had whipped Van den Haute along turned into a front wind that fought him. Nobody was there to provide a relay and a respite from the wind. It gets lonely on a long breakaway, the riders complain, with nobody to talk to except the handlebars. The pack picked up its pace. With 10 kilometers to go, the lead was down to 3 minutes 38 seconds. With 5 kilometers to go, it was 2 minutes 28 seconds, with 3 kilometers, 1 minute 35 seconds. The magical time of on the road was over, time indeed had a stop. But Van den Haute was 1 minute 3 seconds ahead at the end of the race and thrilled with his victory, which moved him up to merely eleventh place overall.

A professional rider for nine years, with many campaign ribbons but few medals, Van den Haute turned out to be a graduate of the University of Ghent, entering as a major in chemistry, biology, and physics and graduating with a degree in physical education. "When I was a kid," he said, "there were only two things that mattered to me, music and sports. But my father warned me, 'If you don't want the kind of job that starts at five o'clock in the morning and ends at night, you've got to work at school.'" His biggest triumphs before this day were a victory in the Ghent-Wevelgem classic in 1978 and a stage victory in Paris-Nice in 1984. At age thirty-two, he was in only his third Tour de France.

"It was a nice breakaway," the lone eagle said, "but let's be realistic. I didn't set the world on fire today. Honestly, I know this didn't make me a star."

F I V E

Because Panasonic and Kwantum were

watching each other, worried not so much about victory as about keeping the other from it, the race exploded on what should have been a relaxed cruise back toward Paris. The unlikely match that touched off the powder was Paulo Ferreira, about whom nothing was known except that he was a twenty-two-year-old first-year professional from Portugal, riding for the Sporting Lisbon team.

While the riders were still chatting at the start of the day, at kilometer 3 of the 207-kilometer fifth stage from Béthune to the new city of Cergy-Pointoise, Ferreira broke away. A handful of riders gave desultory pursuit over the next few kilometers, but he managed to build a lead of 1 minute 24 seconds, riding just fast enough to discourage a real counterattack, just slow enough not to raise an alarm. At kilometer 20, Maurice Le Guilloux of La Vie Claire went after the Portuguese. "I rode out like a mailman, waving to the boys and telling them we'd be back soon," the thirty-four-year-old Le Guilloux said later. Three kilometers farther along, Renault showed it intended to control the

57

race by allowing no breakaway to develop without a member of its team along. But it also showed how low it rated this breakaway by sending Vincent Barteau, a twenty-two-year-old second-year professional in his first Tour de France. All three riders were far down in the overall standings, with Barteau leading the two others by more than a minute.

The two neophytes and the veteran joined up at kilometer 26. Listen to Le Guilloux explain how the fifth-longest breakaway in the Tour's eighty-one-year history began: "Barteau wanted to drop back when we had a minute's lead, but I said, 'Let's give it another ten kilometers.' " They moved off and nobody in the pack responded. By kilometer 58 their lead was up to 11 minutes 38 seconds. Thirty kilometers later, as the three rode through Amiens and contested a bonus sprint, the lead was 19 minutes 48 seconds. Barteau won the sprint and the 10,000 francs that went with it, with Le Guilloux second and the unresistant Ferreira third. "Don't let them say I just rested on their wheels during the sprints," he insisted later. "If I didn't fight, it's because I was weary." Ferreira did his share on the relays, though. "He paid his way the last hundred kilometers," Le Guilloux had to admit.

Weather, geography, and politics—everything favored their breakaway. The wind that had been in the riders' faces while they headed north the day before was now at their backs, pushing along anybody who wanted the advantage. Even the countryside was favorable—a series of small hills, the best terrain for splitting the following pack into smaller groups and reducing communications, for allowing the breakaways to be out of sight and out of mind, for giving them the exhilarating feeling of being able to look back and see nobody behind. "It's abnormal to be allowed a twenty-seven-minute lead," Le Guilloux said, referring to their greatest gap, "but if everybody always had a reason to close it up with everybody else, there never would be a breakaway. There's such a thing as tactics and psychological warfare, and that's what happened today." Kwantum and Panasonic were pleased the other team had not escaped, Renault and La Vie Claire had a man in the breakaway, and nearly everybody else had an excuse. "We were the only ones, with sometimes Coop, to do anything," said Peugeot's manager, Roland Berland. "If we hadn't done what we did, we would have finished thirty-five minutes behind. But every time we tried to counterattack, we got bogged down in the Kwantum-Panasonic rivalry. Anyway, for us, it was fine to have three men up ahead, picking off the bonus points from Fignon, LeMond, and Hinault."

Three is a fine, nearly perfect, number for a breakaway, since it virtually forces each man to take a turn relaying the others; if one balks at setting the pace and the slipstream, the two others can join and try to leave him behind. Money can also be a factor in deciding whether one rider will relay another, as can friendship; it is not unknown for a rider to relay an opponent who was once a teammate and remains a friend. Often the decision is left to the rider, but his team manager always has the last word. For tactical reasons, he may refuse to allow a relay but order his rider to ride just behind the leader, wearing him down not physically but psychologically.

Three is also a fine number for allowing a deal to be made. "I talked with Barteau," Le Guilloux confessed. "I said to him, 'You take the yellow jersey, let me have the race.' He said he couldn't. That's understandable. Of the three of us, he was the strongest, and you can't really ask a kid of twenty-two to throw away something that big in his first Tour." Le Guilloux was speaking just after the finish. A few hours later he denied that he had offered a deal, but this revised version may be discounted. Riders do barter and even sell races, usually when they feel they have no chance for victory and might as well come out ahead on the day. In any case, neither Le Guilloux nor Barteau tried to make a deal with Ferreira, who spoke no French and seemed to be a beaten man.

As they sped through the sprints, scooping up the bonus times given to the first three finishers, it was either Barteau or Le Guilloux who won, with Ferreira always a complacent third. "It wasn't my job to dynamite things," he said later. Nor was it anybody's job in the pack. More than halfway along a couple of riders went after the breakaways, but the pack was content to have a quiet day and nobody followed. Near the end Renault led a counterattack against the two followers and narrowed their margin, but for nearly 200 kilometers nobody really chased the three breakaways. They finished nearly 18 minutes ahead.

Coming into the long, straight finish, Le Guilloux was resigned to second place as Barteau passed him easily, confident of his victory, when who should suddenly flash by but Ferreira. Pumping furiously, he won by a bicycle length. "The sprint, that's my specialty, after all," he explained through his tears.

"If only somebody had told us the Portuguese could go like that, we would have had some room to maneuver," Le Guilloux complained in *L'Equipe*. "But nobody told us anything. Later I learned he was twelfth yesterday at Béthune. That would have been at least a hint.

"If we wanted to, Barteau and I might have left him behind before the finish, but he was useful in letting us have a breather during the relays. I can tell you that in the final one hundred kilometers he did his part. If only somebody had said we were kidding ourselves, we could have tried something. Barteau had the yellow jersey, he could have given me the stage. I still don't understand what he did to lose it."

Barteau had no answer either. "Of course I'm disappointed," he said. "I wanted the stage. As far as the yellow jersey goes, I don't have any illusions. The stage—I know only too well I won't get another chance soon."

Nobody seemed to be happy except Ferreira, and he kept crying.

The pack came in for bitter criticism for its sluggishness. "What was our position?" asked Walter Godefroot, Kwantum's manager. "We had to watch the Panasonics. With one bonus sprint they take the yellow jersey. When Ferreira was joined by Le Guilloux and Barteau, we said, 'They'll sweep up the points.' I admit the whole thing was bad for cycling, but the behavior of the pack was ridiculous." Panasonic said roughly the same.

At Renault, Laurent Fignon said, "It wasn't good for cycling, but look at those who were responsible. Why should we get involved in the fight between Panasonic and Kwantum? We were sure of getting the yellow jersey."

The emblem of leadership was now worn by the heartbroken Barteau, who had a lead of 1 minute 33 seconds over Le Guilloux. Ferreira was third, 3 minutes 13 seconds behind Barteau. The next closest rider was 17 minutes 45 seconds away from Barteau.

In his ninth Tour, Le Guilloux was known not to be a climber. Barteau wasn't either, said Greg LeMond, his teammate: "He ought to keep the jersey until the mountains, but no longer."

And Ferreira? "What if he's a Portuguese mountain goat?" a television commentator asked. "He's not," everybody answered, feeling moderately confident that this was the truth.

○

Most of the year, Maurice Le Guilloux thought only of others: his wife, his two young daughters, his employer, the Vie Claire bicycle team. At work, he continued to be selfless. He was not a star but an *équipier,* literally "teammate," but actually a support rider, one of the men who earn their living by sacrificing their ambitions in the service of a leader.

At the lowest level, that of *domestique,* the *équipier* fetches and distributes water bottles and raincoats during a race; when the team manager's car is blocked in traffic, the *équipier* will relay instructions to the leader; if the leader has a flat, the *équipier* will give him the wheel from his own bicycle. At a higher level, the *équipier* will be sent after a rival on a breakaway, wearing him down with pursuit, increasing the pace for the riders left behind. At the highest level, the *équipier* rides at the side of his leader, helping him set his rhythm, preceding him up hills so that the leader can save strength by riding in the slipstream of the *équipier*'s bicycle.

Le Guilloux had done all these tasks, and done them well. At the age of thirty-four and after eleven years as a professional, by 1984 he was regarded as a model *équipier.*

"He's a team rider, really fantastic in his loyalty, always doing his job," said Greg LeMond, a former teammate of Le Guilloux's. "He's a devoted team rider, and there's never a problem with him," said Bernard Hinault, a longtime friend and leader to Le Guilloux. "For as long as I can remember, since I've ridden for Bernard I've never started a race with the hope of winning," Le Guilloux said in corroboration.

Sometimes Le Guilloux thought about how he had never won a major race, how he rarely had the opportunity or strength to shine at the end of the day. "I wanted to do something in front of my public," he said a few years ago after a leg of the Tour de France in his native Brittany, "but I didn't have anything left. I have to do an *équipier*'s job, and people don't always understand an *équipier*'s job."

When he thought about this, he also realized that he had become one of the elders of professional racing. How many seasons could be left? He thought especially about the race he had consistently come closest to winning—the 586-kilometer one-day race in May from Bordeaux to Paris. Run partly during the night, Bordeaux-Paris is one of the most demanding of all races. He finished fifth in 1978, third in 1981, and second in 1982. At these times, Le Guilloux, who thought only of others most of the year, allowed himself to think of Le Guilloux. "It's the one race where I can work for myself," he said. "There's no strategy in Bordeaux-Paris, no tactics. It's simply every man for himself." He sat back in his chair and appeared to enjoy the thought during a chat earlier that spring.

Le Guilloux was at his training camp, a hotel in the then forests west of Bordeaux, just beyond the fields and châteaus of the wine country. In its isolation the hotel was perfect as a bus stop for group tours heading to the Atlantic beaches, for businessmen holding weekend seminars, and for a cyclist preparing for an ordeal.

Businesslike, he ticked off the many hours of training he had spent in his week at the hotel before the race. "I did two hundred kilometers on Monday, three hundred and eighty on Tuesday, one hundred on Thursday, and just sixty today"—about twelve hours before the race started, at 2:30 A.M. The training was divided between riding alone and following a motor bicycle; for 358 of its 586 kilometers, Bordeaux-Paris is run behind a motor bicycle, called a *burdin.*

"It's not only long, but hard, and you go so fast," Le Guilloux said. "Behind the *burdin* you can reach sixty-five kilometers an hour, and there's no stopping, never. You just concentrate and pedal," he continued, screwing up his face and hunching his back as his hands reached for imaginary handlebars. "Your feet begin to hurt terribly, and it's impossible to relax. You can't look around or breathe deeply for even fifty meters. The wind changes constantly and you really get buffeted. A house by the side of the road, some trees, they change the wind. And then there's the traffic, the cars and trucks—that's very dangerous.

"And the tedium gets to you. Even eating is difficult. You're sitting down and you need the kind of food that takes two hours to get from here"—he sliced at his throat—"to here"—he jabbed at his stomach. "I'll tell you, it's so difficult that all you want to do is win.

"I've spent three months preparing for the race, I've sacrificed so many chances to win small races in Brittany and make some money.

The team has spent so much money on me. But if I knew that I would finish third in this Bordeaux-Paris, I'd leave right now and go straight home.

"So why do I want to do it?" he repeated the question. "For the glory. More for the glory than for the sport or the money. What does the winner make? Ten thousand francs" (actually 17,000 francs).

"It's the last great race," Le Guilloux said. "It's an inhuman race —the distance, the hardship, the danger. People love to watch it. It's the last legendary race, and a chance for me to become part of the legend."

Le Guilloux didn't mention it, but he was also seeking revenge. After his second place in Bordeaux-Paris in 1982, he had no doubt that his team, then Renault, would enter him in 1983. Instead, while he was riding in the Tour of Spain, he learned that he had been passed over for a younger rider.

"I have no illusions left," Le Guilloux said then. "This was the chance of my career.

"I have to avoid thinking too much about it because I'm in Spain to help Bernard Hinault and I don't have the right to waste my energy. If I give in to the blues, I'd have to believe my career has just ended."

At the end of the season, Le Guilloux joined Hinault in leaving Renault and moving to a new team, La Vie Claire. When Hinault called a press conference to announce the team, Le Guilloux was present, bursting to talk about another chance at Bordeaux-Paris.

Intensive training began in March. Le Guilloux was set back by an attack of nephritis that put him in the hospital for a week in April and took 11 pounds off his six-foot 165-pound frame.

"Despite all this, he's in good shape," said Paul Koechli, Le Guilloux's trainer with La Vie Claire. Basing his method on "the physiology of the body," Koechli is a manager of the new school in cycling. Nevertheless, he uses the old-school definition in talking about the Bordeaux-Paris race. "It's a test of perseverance," he said, "a rider knowing his limits and pushing himself right up to that line."

In final preparation, Le Guilloux planned a late lunch, then a massage, and then he hoped to nap. "It's difficult to sleep the evening before this race," he said. "I always try, but I haven't succeeded yet.

Instead, I pack my things, concentrate my thoughts, and pray for good weather."

He went in to lunch, sitting with his masseur, his mechanic, and Koechli next to a long table with twenty businessmen discussing that morning's sales seminar and *le marketing.* When his steak arrived, Le Guilloux—just a country boy—startled the businessmen by noisily stropping his knife against his fork.

○

So much for Le Guilloux's prayers: It was raining hard when the twenty riders gathered at 2:00 A.M. to get ready for the race. Nor had he managed to nap. He was intense as he adjusted his heavy uniform for the nightlong ride in the rain.

A few hundred fans stood in the street, mostly jammed against the windows of the Maison du Vin de Bordeaux with its casual display of great bottles of Pauillacs, St.-Emilions, and Médocs. This was the eighty-first running of Bordeaux-Paris, which began in 1891 and was interrupted by the two world wars and, in 1971–1972, by lack of interest. The race was held then in October, at the end of the season, and nobody had the strength to ride all the way to Paris overnight. Once the date was shifted to the late spring, it regained popularity.

At 2:30 the riders moved out in the ceremonial start, and at 3:00 A.M., at a supermarket outside Bordeaux, they left officially. Despite the hour, there were people waiting to cheer them in nearly every small town along the route, a secondary road often paralleling the Paris-Bordeaux superhighway. Most of the fans stood under umbrellas, a few here at a crossroads, which the police had blocked until the riders passed, a few there outside a cluster of houses or a late-night brasserie. In many villages the only spectators were bakers, standing at the curb in their white uniforms, the open doors behind them showing their ovens.

The pace for the first hour, with the riders bunched in the light of trailing cars, was steady at 36 kilometers. It was cold and wet, and soon Koechli's car pulled alongside Le Guilloux to pass him food—rice pudding, chicken ("things that are good for him and that he likes," the trainer explained), bread, cheese ("in a long race you need some fats, not just sugar"), even some baby food ("why not? it's easy to digest"). To wash it down, Le Guilloux had mineral water or tea. As he finished his snack, a signboard announced that Paris was 513 kilometers away.

Rain was still falling as it began to turn light at 5:20. The empty green fields of Chévanceaux, Barbezieux, and Roullet-Saint-Estèphe rolled by. In the village of La Chignole, a farmer stood in his driveway next to two milk cans. By 6:30 the rain had stopped, and by 7:30 the sun was up, and the riders were too hot in their plastic raincoats. One by one, their team cars moved alongside and the riders pulled off clothes and gloves and passed them to hands reaching out the car windows. The UNCP team took advantage of the transfer; a hand reached out a window and settled in the small of a rider's back to push him along. It is a well-practiced trick, and was quickly spotted in the main official's car, if not by the judge riding in each team car. "Stop that, please, the UNCP car," crackled a message on the radio linking all cars. After a few moments, the hand moved out again and settled on the rider. "This is the last warning," the radio announced. The team car dropped back.

Small-town France was awake by this time. In Ruffec, just opening for the day, the butcher stopped loading his small truck with meat for a nearby market day and went to summon his family; two daughters appeared in bathrobes and waved as the cyclists sped by. In the local bar, two men put down their 8:00 A.M. scotch and soda and came outside to cheer. Villagers love bicycle racing, the only sport they can watch free.

At Vivonne, the riders had a 45-minute rest stop, the only one of the race. Sitting in a manor house converted for the day to a training center, the cyclists changed from their bulky night clothing to the shorts and short-sleeved jerseys they would wear the rest of the way. It was time to eat again, and some were content with a yogurt, some with thick sandwiches. Many were rubbing lanolin into the padded crotch of their racing shorts: a long ride lay ahead, and cyclists dread boils. Outside, their bicycles were being tightened and washed, to reduce the chance of grit in the chains and brakes. Inside, the smell of wintergreen was heavy. Le Guilloux, looking concerned, was massaging his feet as the masseur kneaded his thighs.

The crowds were out now along the route, with whole classes of schoolchildren cheering anything that moved, including police cars and television motorcyclists. A great cheer was heard at Poitiers, when the riders, at full speed, fell in behind their pacers on motor bicycles. The trick is to stay close enough to take full advantage of the slipstream—drafting—and the windbreak, and yet never let the bicycle's front wheel touch the machine; at that high speed the bicycle would spin away, out of control. Bicyclist and pacesetter have practiced together for long hours, and the best-coordinated teams looked as if they were attached. A reserve motor bicyclist trailed each tandem as protection for mechanical failure.

Up through the Loire Valley the race continued. It is accepted wisdom that the race does not really start until Orléans—150 kilometers short of Paris—when fatigue begins to separate the riders, but the first sustained breakaway came at Montbazon, 130 kilometers before Orléans.

Marcel Tinazzi of the UNCP team accelerated and quickly built up a 5-minute lead. The winner of this race in 1982, Tinazzi was outspoken as head of the French cyclists' labor union and considered to be a bit of a troublemaker. Whatever the reason, he had not found an employer for the 1984 season and, on France's welfare rolls, had formed his own team—all five riders on relief. He spent his own money to keep the team going, finding a sponsor only two days before the race. As he said later, he had something to prove in Bordeaux-Paris.

Through Orléans and Pithiviers and Milly-la-Forêt, through the departments of Loiret and Seine-et-Marne and Essonne and finally into the last leg, Val-de-Marne—for 275 kilometers Tinazzi kept his lead, the longest breakaway in memory.

With Tinazzi 9 minutes ahead, Le Guilloux began to move up in a counterattack. He was racing well when, at Malesherbes, 87 kilometers from Paris, his back wheel began to crumple. In the few minutes before his bicycle could be repaired by the mechanic in his team car, he had lost his chance to catch Tinazzi. "After that," he said, "I rode without hope."

Close to 4:30 P.M., 13 1/2 hours after he left Bordeaux, Tinazzi cruised alone into the Paris suburb of Fontenay-sous-Bois, the winner by 4 minutes 27 seconds. Hubert Linard of the Peugeot team was second, and Le Guilloux outlasted three rivals for third place. Of the twenty riders who began the race, sixteen finished.

Wan, his face covered with grime, Le Guilloux admitted he was disappointed. "It was an easy race," he said, "except for the rain. I thought I had a good chance until the wheel broke."

Did Le Guilloux remember saying beforehand that if he knew he would finish third he would go straight home? Mercifully, nobody asked that question. Instead, he was asked if he would be back next year to try again. Looking past his questioner, Maurice Le Guilloux chose not to reply.

SIX

*E*specially *in the rain, not much is need-* ed to make a racer fall, not much more than a slick of oil left where a car has been parked or a few wet leaves ready to skid when a tire hits them at an acute angle as the bicyclist leans into a curve. Or the trap may be a cobblestone or streetcar rail polished by decades of use. In Béthune a few days earlier, Sean Kelly, the Irish rider who had dominated the spring races, had gone down hard when his bicycle slipped on a manhole cover. Kelly only skinned his leg, but Jean-Claude Bagot, his teammate with Skil, was less lucky in another fall on the way to Béthune. X rays showed he had fractured his left elbow, and the doctors recommended that he quit the race and allow his arm to be put in a cast for at least three weeks. Bagot refused. This was his first Tour de France, and he wanted to reach Alençon, near his home in Normandy, where his friends would cheer him in. Alencon was only two days away, so the doctors relented and immobilized Bagot's left arm in a heavy bandage.

The next morning, guiding his bicycle with only his right hand, he set off for Cergy-Pontoise. In the first chase after the three breakaways, Bagot began to lose ground on the pack, first 50 meters, then 100, then 300. As the pace slackened, he managed to ride his way back despite considerable pain. With each burst of the pack, Bagot was left behind, and with each drop in the overall speed, he returned, reaching Cergy-Pontoise only 3 minutes late. "I had a terrible time," he admitted. "All I hope for now is to make it to Alençon for my friends' sake. Afterward . . ."

Even on a dry and hot day there are falls. There is not much space to maneuver when 170 riders are traveling together and the slightest narrowing of the road squeezes them even closer. Handlebars bump, wheels and pedals graze, and down goes the rider, who is locked into his pedals with toe clamps. Usually the damage is no worse than a strawberry on a knee or thigh, rating not even a mention in the daily medical communiqué by the Tour's three doctors. Sometimes the damage seems worse, but isn't. When the race poured off the main street in Louvroil and around a corner into a smaller street, Alfonso Florez, a Colombian, was jostled and fell hard. His face obscured by blood from the split in his head, he barely managed to finish; the next morning he was jaunty again.

Unlike in the movies, nobody ever falls because an opponent has pushed a tire pump into his wheel at high speed. This just isn't done, and not only because professional bicyclists believe in live and let live; everybody rides on a team, and vengeance would be swift. There can be roughness in the final sprint to the finish, but not back here at kilometer 97 of the 202-kilometer ride to Alençon. Here the major problem is inattention, the mind wandering to thoughts of home and glory, the eye wandering to the beauties of field or sky. The riders may be deep in conversation about politics, women, the idiocy of team managers, or any of the hundreds of things people talk about instead of concentrating on their work.

A rider does not have to be clumsy to fall, but it helps. Joaquim Agostinho was indeed clumsy and fell often. "If he had a brick for every fall, what a castle he could have built," a friend said affectionately about Agostinho a few weeks before the 1984 Tour de France and a few weeks after he fell in the Tour of the Algarve in his native Portugal. As a tribute in L'Equipe pointed out, it was to be the last fall for the world champion faller. He was in a coma in Lisbon, clinically dead for nearly two weeks, until his life-support system was turned off.

At age forty-one, Agostinho had been preparing for the Tour de France by riding in the Tour of the Algarve far south of Lisbon. In the fifth stage, 300 meters from the finish, a dog darted into the road and the bicyclists veered and braked, many of them colliding and falling. Agostinho was easy to pick out in the mass on the ground since he was wearing the yellow jersey of the overall leader. Holding his head, he rose and climbed back on his bicycle. Two riders supported him on either side as he wobbled across the finish line. Then he was taken to a nearby hotel and put to bed with an icepack on his head. Later he was taken to a clinic in Faro and then sped by ambulance to Lisbon for brain surgery, nine hours after his fall. He lapsed into the coma during the ambulance ride.

Agostinho was respected and even loved in the cycling world. He was, as they say, a man of the Tour de France, finishing eighth in his debut in 1969, fourteenth in 1970, fifth in 1971, eighth in 1972 and 1973, sixth in 1974, fifteenth in 1975, thirteenth in 1977, third in 1978 and 1979, and fifth in 1980. In 1981, far behind and suffering, he quit the race during a mountain stage, pulling off the road with what was generally described as an attack of nerves, although he would not discuss it publicly. After a year out of competition, he returned to his Sem team in 1983 and finished eleventh in the Tour. Then he went home to Portugal and helped form the Sporting Lisbon team, with which he planned to race in the Tour de France in 1984.

He was not a winner but a competitor. "I'm not made to win," he said. "To be a winner, you sometimes have to know how to climb over people. I don't know how to do that. If I tried, I'd fall."

He fell anyway. One of his worst spills came in 1979 at a traffic island outside the city of Saint-Brieuc in Brittany. When the Tour left the next morning, Agostinho was covered with bandages but still riding, and a week later he won the arduous mountain stage at L'Alpe-d'Huez. He was durable, as could be expected of a former shepherd who began his racing career at twenty-five because he first served three years in combat with the Portuguese army in Angola. "Cycling is tough," the tribute in *L'Equipe* recalled his saying, "but what is it compared to war? You worry every day about being killed. For three years in Angola I saw my buddies die alongside me three or four times a week. But I'm a survivor. My job was at the front, setting up ambushes. It was them or me. The Tour de France is less dangerous.

"But I don't like to make comparisons like that, I don't like to think about the war. It taught me to endure suffering. It was during night marches that I built my muscles and my heart. For a long time I had to fight for my life or a piece of meat. After that, L'Alpe-d'Huez. . . ."

Or even the flat road to Alençon during the sixth stage in this Tour de France. Ten kilometers from the finish there was another mass fall and down went Jean-Claude Bagot despite his precautions to protect his left arm. "I was careful to keep five meters behind everybody else, but when they all went down, I couldn't help myself. With my left arm immobilized it was impossible to avoid everybody spilled on the road." Again he finished the day's stage; this time the X rays showed that he had broken his right elbow. With both arms plastered, he went home the next day.

Pulling out with him was Serge Beucherie, a Frenchman with the Peugeot team, another victim of the mass crash. Like the twenty or thirty other riders involved, Beucherie got back on his bicycle and finished while his team manager shouted encouragement from the window of his car. Team managers are eager to keep a man in the race with more than two weeks to go, but Beucherie was unable to continue: the doctors found that he had pedaled 10 kilometers on a broken left leg.

"What's awful about bicycling," Greg LeMond said, "is that you're supposed to get up, get back on your bike, and finish. In any other sport they'd let you lie there for a while. What if you'd done something to your neck and they get you up and put you on your bike and break your neck and you're paralyzed the rest of your life?" A month before the Tour de France, LeMond fell during an exhibition race in the Netherlands. He promised his wife he would wear a helmet during the Tour but he didn't, complaining that it was too hot. In Europe, helmets are compulsory for bicyclists only in the Benelux countries, and nobody wears them elsewhere.

In addition to their being much hotter than the cloth cap bicyclists wear, the usual complaint about helmets is that their protective value has not been proven. Besides, people like to say, few bicyclists have been killed or seriously hurt in crashes. In addition to Agostinho, the list includes Camille Danguillaume, who was bowled over and killed by a press motorcycle during the Championship of France in 1950; Serge Coppi, who died after a fall in the Tour of Piedmont in 1951; Marc

Hulart, who succumbed to injuries after running into a car in the Grand Prix of Fourmies in 1962; and José Samyn, who died after colliding with a program seller at an exhibition race in Belgium in 1969.

Then there was Paul Jesson. In 1979 he was an amateur rider in his second year of European competition after moving to Belgium from his native New Zealand. "I won six races as an amateur, but I wasn't well known," he explained during that year's Tour de France. The Splendor team, one of the weaker ones, had been unable to sign a tenth rider for the race and, in one of those dreams that fill the heads of amateur riders throughout Europe, turned to Jesson just days before the Tour. His first race as a professional was in the prologue, and he finished respectably enough in the middle of the pack. So little known was he that the official statistics listed him under the name of Christian Jezzon. "It's Jesson, with two 'esses,' and my first name is Paul," he insisted over breakfast in Deauville before a day's stage, as a teammate, Sean Kelly, nodded confirmation. Jesson had not been expected to survive the first day on the road, when the Tour de France entered the Pyrenees for three mountain stages, but he had come through and was proud of it. "Everybody said it was the first time I even saw a mountain," he complained. "But it wasn't. In Christchurch, when I lived in New Zealand, we had mountains. I knew what a mountain was, it was just that I had never cycled up one before."

Like Bagot and so many other riders, Jesson's goal was not to win but simply to finish, to make it home. "What I want," he said, "is to make it back to Belgium. I've got friends there and I want them to see me." He made it that far, but a year later, coming around a curve in a spring race, he collided with a car that somehow had evaded the policemen closing the road. Jesson lost a leg in the accident and now works as a garage mechanic in Belgium. "He comes out to see a race sometimes, but you can never guess when," Kelly said. "He's a very bitter man. It's understandable, isn't it?"

○

Hours after the sixth stage into Alencon was over, Sean Kelly was kept busy explaining what had happened in the final 20 meters of the sprint finish. Kelly had seemed to veer and impede Gilbert Glaus as the Swiss rider tried to pass Kelly on the right along the iron barriers set up to keep spectators off the course. The Irishman insisted he had blocked

Glaus within the rules, which are as much unwritten as otherwise.

"Sprinters bounce you around," Jacques Anquetil commented from his experiences as a five-time winner of the Tour de France. "That's why I skipped sprints." They bump and pull jerseys and swerve, and sometimes they help a teammate by taking his hand and giving him a crack-the-whip pull, a trick they learn in track racing, where it is legal. In road racing it is illegal, but so are most of the practices used in a final sprint, and they are rarely punished. The general feeling is that sprinters need all the help they can get.

Sprinting is a skill and therefore can be developed, including the use of a protector to lead the sprinter in close to the finish, letting him save his strength by drafting. But it is also a gift, starting with the right type of body, usually compact and well-muscled, especially in the thighs, where runners and bicyclists get the power to surge for a short distance. Strong nerves, or a lack of imagination, are also needed to overcome the thought of what a spill would mean just ahead of the pack. There are not many thoroughbred sprinters, those who can be counted on to finish consistently among the first seven or eight, where the going is roughest and the pace fastest. Behind this elite group are the sprinters who consistently finish eighth to, say, fifteenth, taking few risks, since in gang finishes the same time is given to all riders passing the line with no more than a second's gap among them; seventy or eighty riders can finish in a file nearly 100 meters long and all be recorded in the same time, although the winner was clear-cut.

Few sprinters are more than specialists, and some of them manage even to sound proud when they discuss how poorly they will do in the mountains. Kelly was not one of these. A first-class sprinter, he was a good time trialist and an improving climber, as he could prove by the green jersey he had won for overall points during the preceding two Tours de France. The green jersey is a coveted one, and its wearer must be able to score points on all terrain, as Kelly did when he won the jersey in 1982 while taking five daily stages and again in 1983 when he won none but finished close enough to gain points. In 1984 he had the sort of spring riders dream about: first in Paris-Roubaix, first in the Critérium International, first in Paris-Nice, first in Liège-Bastogne-Liège, second in Milan-San Remo, second in the Tour of Flanders. At age twenty-eight he was clearly at a peak. His efforts were pointed toward the Tour de France, but nothing had gone right for him since the start. First there was the fall in Béthune, and now, in Alençon, the incident with Glaus.

"Kelly interfered with me, and he did it deliberately," Glaus charged. He accused Kelly of leaving his line, the unmarked lane each rider is entitled to, when he realized Glaus was passing on his right. Long-faced and defensive, Kelly tried to fend off the charges. "He's accusing me of blocking him, but a sprinter has to know how to close the door, doesn't he?" He insisted that he had not seen Glaus and even that he would have let Glaus through if only he had called out. Finally Kelly said the barricades had been improperly placed and had jutted into the road, forcing Glaus in.

The judges watched the television replays, which showed the near-bumping and Glaus throwing up his left arm in the traditional sign of official protest as Kelly sped on, leaning forward on his bicycle and losing by half a wheel's length to Franck Hoste, who was just starting to throw up both his arms in the traditional sign of victory. The judges ruled that Kelly had interfered with Glaus and dropped the Irishman from second place to last in the pack, 140th in this case but still in the same time as the winner. They also fined Kelly 1,000 francs and penalized him 15 seconds in overall time plus the points he would have won toward the green jersey.

The judges acted quickly, perhaps remembering a similar finish in 1983, when Henk Lubberding, a Dutchman with the Raleigh team, unmistakably bumped Michel Laurent, a Frenchman with Coop, into the barriers, sending the rider one way and his bicycle another. Lubberding had not simply tried to close the door; during their long two-man breakaway, Laurent had refused to relay him and stayed right on his rear wheel, the classic wheel-sucker, or parasite, as cyclists call such a rider. Lubberding's anger visibly mounted with each kilometer as he was forced to do the work to keep the breakaway alive. By far a faster finisher than Laurent, Lubberding should have sprinted away in the last 100 meters, but he was hambound with frustration and rage. When Laurent began to pass him, the Dutchman exploded and banged him into the railing. Lubberding finished first and was disqualified, with the victory given to Laurent, who staggered across the finish line carrying his bicycle (the rules specify that a rider must finish with his bicycle to have his time made official but not that he must be riding it).

○

Kelly's disqualification moved Glaus up to only third place, but he seemed pleased. Injured in his wallet and his general classification, Kelly suffered most in his morale, he said later that night, pitching pebbles disconsolately at a target only he could see. "A car can't run on two spark plugs," he complained. "If it does, it doesn't go too well. My morale has taken a terrible hammering. It wouldn't take much to get me to pack my bags and go home."

Kelly was a long way from home, either the apartment he keeps near Brussels during the racing season or the farm where he was born in Carrick-on-Suir in the Republic of Ireland. Those who have been there know it as a working farm of about forty acres, with dirt floors in the house, the sort of farm that Irishmen say spawns men of the people, like Kelly. The Irish like to tell Kelly stories; how the obstetrician told his mother, "Mrs. Kelly, your baby has the finest muscle tone of any I've delivered"; how the young Kelly belonged to a bicycling club too poor to sponsor a race because it did not have the money to buy medals for the winners, and how, hearing this news, Kelly rode home, packed a sack, returned to his club and, pouring his medals and trophies onto the table, asked, "Here, will these do for Sunday?"

The Irish tell of Kelly's race with a schoolboys team, ages thirteen and fourteen, against a juniors team, ages fifteen to seventeen, with all the difference in strength and skill that the age difference implies. Kelly was the only schoolboy able to keep up with the juniors, but five minutes into the race he pulled up and waited for his teammates because, see, he was just a lad and a lonely one too and maybe, just maybe, it was the last time Kelly ever lost his nerve. And then there's the story how, joining one of Ireland's top amateur teams, he was asked if he would work for the leader and he replied, "Sure I'll work for him, provided he'll keep up with me."

The likable Kelly was too quiet to tell them himself, but the stories went on and on. How he was selected for Ireland's bicycling team at the 1976 Olympic Games in Montreal but first raced in South Africa, smart enough to use a false name but dumb enough to think he could evade the sports blacklist for competing in South Africa. How he was suspended and went instead to France, where he joined an amateur team in Metz, getting 250 francs a month for the food he cooked in the corner of a furniture exhibition hall that was curtained off for his living quarters. How he won eighteen of twenty-five races for his club, how he went home for the winter, and how Viscount Jean de Gribaldy flew over to Ireland in his private plane and, negotiating with Kelly in the mud of the farmyard, offered him a professional contract that Kelly was only too pleased to accept if the viscount would only double the money involved, which the viscount was clever enough to do.

For all this, Kelly's development as a professional was slow. When he swept the spring races in 1984, he was able to say truthfully that he might be twenty-eight years old but that he felt much younger, since he had spent his first three years as a professional not doing much more than watching and learning. By 1982, he had his five stage victories and green jersey in the Tour, and by the next year, when he won the Tour of Switzerland, he seemed to have mastered the mountains. With Hinault out of the Tour de France in 1983, Kelly should have been a strong favorite, but he seemed uncertain whether to go for the yellow jersey or the green, whether to disperse his energies by collecting points in the road sprints and intermediate climbs. Few riders—most recently Hinault in 1979 and Eddy Merckx in 1971 and 1972—have the strength and all-around ability to win both jerseys by competing for points at climbs and sprints as well as riding a tactical race for overall victory.

Probably not even Kelly can say whether his apparent indecision affected him when he put on the yellow jersey in 1983 in Pau at the foot of the Pyrenees. But the next day he had a bad stage in the mountains, losing enough minutes that the yellow jersey was out of sight. He took over the green jersey and wore it the rest of the way to Paris.

In 1984, after his great start, he announced that the green jersey no longer interested him. He should have been a strong favorite again, but the doubts remained about his ability in the highest mountains. "Sometimes he climbs so darn well you can't understand why he gets dropped in the Tour," Greg LeMond said. "But he does."

The mountains were still four days away, though, and Kelly had other things to worry about. More than twenty minutes down in the overall standings and without a stage victory in the Tour since 1982, he was talking in Alençon about morale. "If it isn't there, there's nothing the cyclist can do," he said. "The time trial will be decisive for me. It should show me what my possibilities are." He didn't sound hopeful.

SEVEN

*A*fter 7 days and 946 kilometers, the Tour de France was ready to begin. Vincent Barteau and his two companions in the Cergy-Pontoise breakaway might be ahead of the field by up to 17 minutes, but their lead was not to be taken seriously; a day in the mountains could easily eat up a lead of a quarter of an hour. The real contenders began with the fourth-place rider, Phil Anderson of the Panasonic team, who was separated by less than a minute and a half from the twenty-eighth-place rider, Bernard Hinault. Between these two were such favorites as Laurent Fignon in tenth place and Greg LeMond in eleventh place. Even Sean Kelly, far, far back in 109th place, was only 3 minutes 26 seconds behind Anderson.

The favorite in the individual time trial, the seventh stage, was of course Hinault, who had won twelve of these races, not counting his dominance in the prologues, in his Tour de France career. The excitement, the opportunity to outride his challengers, to leave them minutes behind in what amounts to a man-to-man duel, were expected to bring out the best, as usual, in Hinault—the Badger, backed into a corner, gets a chance to show his teeth and break free.

The individual time trial, where each rider leaves at regular intervals in inverse order of overall ranking, is generally considered to be not only the most demanding part of a stage race but also the most liberating in its simplicity. Cooperation is banned: If there are no relays to be gotten, there are none to be given. There is not even that vague quality, team spirit, to egg anybody on. Each rider races only the clock. The ideal time trialist is that legendary rider, the exceedingly stupid but strong one—the French say he's Belgian, the Belgians say he's Dutch, the Dutch say he's French—who needs to be told during a road stage, "Speed up now" or "Slow down now." In an individual time trial all he needs is somebody to keep shouting, "Faster, faster."

This is not fair, for what the time trialist really needs is concentration, a sense of tunnel vision for a constant 20 or 30 meters over a course that can vary between 40 and 70 kilometers. He needs to understand the rhythm of the course and how to make his strength last. The ability to bear pain, knowing how to suffer, is also vital. No relaxation is permitted, no unnecessary coasting around a curve or down a hill, no yielding to the urge to shift the body or sit up straight for a while as the shoulders and back become cramped from holding the same position, no accepting the temptation to take a breather once a rider has caught the man who left 2 minutes before him.

His back may be aching, his lungs bursting, and his legs wobbly from a buildup of lactic acid in his muscles; still he must pedal on, knowing how to suffer. "I was just fine for forty kilometers, but I did the last ten kilometers just seeing black," the Irish rider Stephen Roche said later. He blamed the bonk, that sudden emptiness from hunger that riders guard against by filling the back pockets of their jerseys with fruit and pastries. Some, however, underestimate the amount of food they should bring along, and some even forget to eat what they have, so deeply are they concentrating on the 20 meters ahead. In a road stage, a teammate can share his food; in the individual time trial this is forbidden. Then the sugar in the rider's blood gives out under the exertion, and at best, like Roche, he sees black or begins wobbling or visibly loses power. The bonk, also called the knock, a noun and even a verb, is not as elegant a name as the French give it, a *fringale.* Or, as they say in this part of Normandy, an empty sack won't stand up.

All along the 67 kilometers from Alençon to Le Mans the road was spotted with spectators, not simply the casual types expected on a crisp and sunny day, but the ones who came out with a camp stool, a stopwatch, and notepads, who timed each contender at that particular spot and then shouted out to a rival how much ahead or behind he was. Swept away on the breeze, the words were rarely heard by the riders, but the spectator, the true believer, felt he had done his service for the sport. Even if they heard the times, many riders considered the information pointless since they were going at top speed, or felt they were. For some riders this was comparatively slow, and they might finish 10 minutes behind. Time trialing is a matter of sustained, not finishing, speed. Since this can be taught along with concentration and even the ability to suffer, time trialing is a discipline where great improvement is possible. An average climber can work in the mountains in the off-season, reconnoitering the highest Alps, climbing them time and time again to lose his fear that he can never make it to the top in a good time; but climbing is a gift, strongly dependent on lung capacity, and so climbing ability can never be vastly improved. Sprinting is both a gift and a skill, and time trialing is almost purely a skill. Laurent Fignon finished sixteenth in the first time trial of the 1983 Tour and was a clear winner in the last of four. He was wearing the yellow jersey then and was full of willpower, which may be the one word that says it all about time trialing.

On the course the fans were yelling at Kelly that he was nearly a minute and a half ahead of the pace set by Martín Ramírez, a Colombian with the Système U team and the only good time trialist to have set off before the Irishman. Kelly didn't need their information because, he said later, he knew he was doing well. The course was ideal for him, with many ups and downs and a few long hills. With his ability to accelerate on a slight ascent, he much preferred this run to a flat course. His strong legs pumping as he stood on the climb, he kept passing riders who had left many minutes before him. At first they were a speck atop a distant hill, then recognizably a man on a bicycle followed by a team car, then an easily identifiable number, and then they were behind. The rules forbade drafting on an opponent's wheel, but Kelly had no desire to rest. "I called my wife and she said that if I didn't do well, she'd divorce me," Kelly joked afterward. By then he had finished in 1 hour 27 minutes 49 seconds and was leading the field. His time was far superior to that of riders who had started in the lower end, as he had, but as the stronger riders finished, it seemed as if he might win his first stage of the Tour de France since 1982.

Looking gaunt, Hinault finished 33 seconds behind Kelly, good enough for second place so far, with Roche third, 41 seconds behind. Most of the other specialists were a minute or two behind. Some had the excuse of age or injury: Joop Zoetemelk, Jan Raas, and Gerrie Knetemann—the only riders ever to have beaten Hinault in a time trial —were all in their thirties, and Raas and Knetemann had been badly hurt in crashes the last two years. Jean-Luc Vandenbroucke of La Redoute went head over heels 3 kilometers from the start when his experimental bicycle broke in two under him; he grabbed a replacement from his team car and finished 6 minutes 48 seconds down, bleeding badly from the temple and shoulder. With the excuse of a bad cold, LeMond had a disappointing day, coming in nearly 2 minutes behind Kelly. Most were waiting in the arrival area, explaining the day away, when it was announced that Fignon was clearly in the lead at an intermediate point and closing fast.

Kelly and Hinault ride a time trial on power, LeMond and Roche on class, the riders' word for "grace," and Fignon on a combination of the two. By now everybody had noticed how much stronger he looked than he had the year before, how he gave an impression of force. He seemed to have added ten pounds to his body, mainly in the shoulders and thighs, although his form had been difficult to judge before today. Was he just the Invisible Man, as some called him after his victory in 1983, a rider who outlasted a race without Hinault, or was he a dominant rider? Today was a chance to find out.

For the time trial, Renault had provided its team with specially streamlined bicycles and aerodynamic helmets. Fignon used both pieces of equipment, although he remained cautious afterward about how much they had helped. They had not hurt: he streamed through the finish 16 seconds ahead of Kelly. Nobody else came close.

Interviewed on television, Hinault was gracious enough to tell Fignon, "My reign has ended, now it's your turn." Nobody was sure whether he meant only in the individual time trials, and it did no good to press him. "One day doesn't make a race," Hinault snapped from the depths of the trailer his team kept for his hideaway. At least a few other riders tended to agree with him. Yes, said Knetemann, the respected Dutch rider with the Europ Décor team, Fignon had impressed everybody. "But there are still two weeks to go, and in the Tour de France anything can happen. So be careful. Don't bury Hinault just yet."

Fignon was not making that mistake, although he was sounding confident. "I needed to ride a strong race," he said, "but that was better than I'd hoped for." He was flanked by his mother and father, who had come over to Le Mans for the day, and it was easy to see him not as a defending champion in the world's greatest bicycle race but as a boy still young enough to need a bit of consolation from his parents this afternoon in case he had been beaten badly.

○

The next to last time he saw Paris, Alain Meslet's heart was neither young nor gay but troubled. He had just admitted that he had thrown bicycle races and used illegal drugs, and then, the day after his public confession, there he was riding in the Tour, completing the traditional last laps on the Champs-Elysées and finishing forty-first overall in the 1981 race.

At the end of the afternoon, while hundreds of thousands of Frenchmen were cheering Bernard Hinault's third victory, Meslet, then thirty-one years old, retired. His six-year career as a professional ended on the broad and chic avenue where he had known his only real glory: in 1977 he had won the final stage in Paris, crossing the finish line with arms upraised and the sly smile of somebody who has surprised even himself.

The final day's winner is always eclipsed by the finish of the long haul and the anointing of the overall champion; even the daily victory ceremony in which the stage winner is given a bouquet is usually overlooked while some French dignitary presents a porcelain vase to the overall winner. So Meslet's victory was unsung. But it mattered a great deal to him.

"I used to make between 1,500 francs and 1,800 francs in each of the critériums," the exhibition races staged throughout the country for weeks after the Tour de France. "In 1977, because of that victory, I reached 2,500 francs, which wasn't bad," he said.

Money meant a lot to Meslet. As a professional bicycle rider with four teams, he sometimes was willing to do anything to make money, as he admitted just before the Tour ended. Then he slipped away, opening a bicycle shop in his native Brittany—"turning a page," as he put it.

Meslet returned to Paris when the 1982 Tour de France completed its journey from Basel, Switzerland. Instead of traveling by bicycle, he arrived by car, driving for *Le Télégramme,* a daily newspaper in Brest, a city in Brittany near his home in the village of Evron.

Brittany is big cycling territory, so *Le Télégramme* devotes pages every day to the Tour and sends along two reporters to cover its every moment. Under the French journalists' union contract, they are entitled to a driver, and by chance Meslet was chosen to chauffeur them, picking his way with horn and occasionally brake through the pack. He shadowed the riders from town to town—moving around them to reach advance observation posts or restaurants, staying at their heels until the finish, when while the reporters scrambled from the car and trusted Meslet to park it, unpack it, and prepare it for the next day's chase.

With more than 300 reporters following the Tour by car, not to mention two or three vehicles for each team, plus innumerable cars for officials, there is plenty of employment available for drivers. No special training is needed, since job requirements exactly fit the average French motorist: disregard for speed limits, contempt for others on the road, and heartfelt trust in immortality. Many of the drivers had been involved with the Tour before as riders, and now sat behind the wheel as a way of staying in touch.

Jean-Claude Theillière, for example, was a professional racer for eight years, and rode in the Tour for four years as a teammate of Jacques Anquetil in the late 1950s and 1960s. Theillière, who now owns a printing shop in the central city of Clermont-Ferrand, has been a driver for the press for five years. "I applied years ago," he said, "and then one day they called and said I had the job. They pay me, of course, or else I would spend July at the seashore, but it's still nice to be back with the Tour."

Theillière never won a stage, but like Meslet he once had a day to remember. In 1966 Theillière won the French championship. He keeps the jersey—blue, white, and red, "silk, you know"—in a closet at home and shows it occasionally to friends. "It's a nice souvenir," he says.

Meslet does not have a similar souvenir, but he came close. "My biggest regret was the championship of France in 1976 at Montauban," he has said. He finished second because, he admitted, he threw the race for money.

Meslet revealed this in 1981, just before he retired, in an interview with the respected Noël Couëdel for the newspaper *L'Equipe.* The interview caused no stir because the next day Hinault won the race again, and for weeks everybody was discussing little else but the man in the yellow jersey.

Since then Meslet had dropped out of general sight. His presence in the race as a chauffeur seemed to have caused no adverse comment. "I still have a lot of friends among the riders," he insisted. "Nobody is nasty to me because of what I said." He got his chauffeur's job, he continued, when *Le Télégramme* phoned and invited him to work. "Of course I said yes. I like the Tour and meant it no harm. I said what had to be said, what I needed to say."

"What you're saying," Couëdel asked, "you're saying out of rancor?"

"Not at all," Meslet contended. "I'm happy to say it because young racers don't pay attention."

"You quit cycling happy?"

"Oh yes, very. Without cycling, I would have wound up working in a factory."

Nobody has publicly challenged what Meslet said, so it can be inferred that he spoke truthfully. He asserted that he spoke for many other riders.

Discussing the 1976 championships, Meslet said, "I was racing with Guy Sibille, who was smarter than me. He offered me a lot of money to let him win. I was starting to build a house and was making twenty-five hundred francs a month, so I was taking a big risk. I accepted the offer of money. I'm sorry to have sold out . . . Instead of the money I got, between the critériums and salary increase, I could have made four times that by winning the championship. I made a mistake."

"Sibille got the best of you, but later you did the same to others," said Couëdel.

"Naturally," Meslet replied. "You have to be cold-blooded and not worry about making friends. I've sold races, but that happens often enough. Last year [1980], for example, I sold my services to anybody who wanted them. I was racing well on the Côte d'Azur and in the Tour of the Tarn, but you've got to be a realist. Those are only second-rank races. I wasn't selling the championship of France.

"I wasn't winning enough and I needed money. Cycling is a nice way to make your living, but it can be deceiving. The sport I like is track and field. It's healthy, it's pleasant to watch and it hasn't been ruined by money."

Then Meslet spoke about the use of drugs. "In 1976," Couëdel said, "you were astonished that nobody noticed you had gained a lot of weight during the Tour de France."

"That's right, I remember," Meslet answered. "I trusted the way we were prepared for the race. But in the first stage, I finished in the last five. Something had gone wrong. That night I felt like my skin was cracking. I looked in the mirror and got scared. I was swelling up as I watched.

"I know I was to blame too, because I accepted all that stuff, including vitamin potions with the labels scratched off. I needed money. I was young. I was dazzled by good results. But finally I understood that my health was worth more than all that. In 1977 I took care of myself. It's better to be a minor racer than to burn up inside. Cortisone, there's the enemy.

"What I've got to say is simply this: Pay attention to your health. Don't take cortisone, it stays in the body. All that saved me is that I was stupid for only a short time."

At the end of the interview, Couëdel said that "people are going to say that . . . you and I give a bad impression of cycling."

"Perhaps," Meslet said. "But you have to understand that everything I've said, a lot of riders think but hesitate to say. I assure you that many riders think like me, but nobody talks about it. When they're asked, they tell lies. What I've said is the truth."

So Meslet continues to insist. "Nobody holds it against me," he said one morning while he was a chauffeur, waiting for the race to start. "There were no reprisals after the interview, and here I am, back with the Tour."

The bicycle racers set off, and Meslet excused himself. It was time to slip behind the wheel of the car and follow the pack to Paris. By 1983 he was gone as a chauffeur and nobody from *Le Télégramme* would say where or why. The next year Meslet returned, briefly, during the time trial in Le Mans, wandering through the press room and the finishing area, just wanting to say hello to the boys—at least to those who remembered him.

EIGHT

So many happy faces the next morning.
Sean Kelly had vaulted into eighteenth place overall, not quite four minutes behind Laurent Fignon, and was feeling just dandy. Vincent Barteau had lost more than five minutes to Fignon in the individual time trial but had gained on Maurice Le Guilloux, now leading him by more than three minutes, and on Paulo Ferreira, leading him by nearly ten, so he was more secure than ever in the yellow jersey and felt fine too. Fignon was in fourth place overall, only three minutes behind Ferreira, so he felt good. Even Bernard Hinault had the consolation of moving up to sixth place overall, just a minute and a half behind Fignon.

The long face in the crowd before the 192-kilometer ride from Le Mans to Nantes, the eighth stage, belonged to Greg LeMond. With a week of the Tour past, he had done nothing to justify his reputation, and he knew it. Coughing heavily, he said after the time trial, "I didn't expect to do well. I didn't feel strong, and I wasn't. All you have to do is lose a second a kilometer and you're out of it." His teammates might still speak of LeMond and Fignon as coleaders, but LeMond did not seem so certain. "It's a three-week race," he said after the time trial, "but if Fignon keeps doing times like this and I keep doing times like this, he'll be the leader."

LeMond blamed a cold he had caught in the north, where his bedroom had not been air conditioned, as few are in France, and soon he was complaining about the corns his racing shoes were giving him. Another pair of shoes was being rushed to him. Nobody disbelieved

LeMond, who was not a complainer, but as some riders pointed out, he did have a contract with a shoe manufacturer, and he really was too experienced a rider to have started the Tour with the wrong shoes, wasn't he? The real trouble with the American, they said, was how distracted he had allowed himself to become when his mind should have been on racing. He was shadowed each morning and night by American television crews, who recorded the private details of his life in the race, just one more take each night as they tucked him into bed and another each morning as he arose. They filmed him eating, even shaving; they filmed him with his teammates and his family. When he visited the medical truck to have his feet treated, the television cameras moved in for a close-up. When he crossed the finish line glassy-eyed, a television camera was the first to greet him, beating even the team mechanic with a towel and a bottle of Perrier.

Alors, LeMond and the television crews were Americans, and this was the American way, not unconnected to the dollar, many dollars. Gone were the days of LeMond the cowboy, posing in a publicity photograph for Renault in an improbable ten-gallon hat while holding a horse on which, even more improbably, sat Hinault on a recruiting mission to Nevada. Now it was LeMond the businessman, as in Fignon's springtime remark that he wouldn't be surprised to see LeMond leave Renault someday soon for a team offering more money. Guilelessly LeMond fostered this image. Fignon had often complained about the low salaries bicycle racers made in relation to tennis players, but always without naming names or specifying figures. LeMond had done his research: "Jack Nicklaus figures to make three million a year from his industries," he would say during an interview, "and Ivan Lendl made one and a half million last year just in winnings." This kind of talk was likely to be misunderstood in a sport where the average athlete hoped only to open a bicycle shop in his hometown when he retired. "But the real money is over the long haul," LeMond would continue. "One way is to build a golf course and put up homes all around it." The American! they said in a country where membership, not ownership, in a golf club must be revealed on the income tax form as a sign of hidden wealth.

So, without victory LeMond's isolation was growing. Fignon tried to be solicitous: "I rode well. Another day, maybe Greg will be the one in top shape. For now, nothing has changed. There are still two leaders of our team. We'll keep riding that way." Cyrille Guimard, the Renault team manager, confirmed this. "Obviously Greg's morale suffered in the time trial. He realizes how much is expected of him and, added to that pressure, he's worried about his health. He needs to have something good happen to him."

Instead, the good things kept happening to people near LeMond, like his teammate Pascal Jules, who took advantage of the continuing feud between the Dutch teams Kwantum and Panasonic to win the day's ride, Renault's fourth victory in eight days. The team was capitalizing on the situation, obeying Guimard's dictum just before the start: "There are two ways for a team to ride in the Tour. Either you control the race or you let the others do it. When we had Hinault, we were strong enough to do it the first way. Now there are other factors, and you can win the race with a weak team, as we did in 1976, or lose it with a strong one."

Guimard did not speak from experience about losing the Tour with a strong team. Since 1976, when he had retired from racing at the age of twenty-nine and took over the Gitane team, which later became Renault, he had managed three winners of six Tours de France: Lucien Van Impe in his first year, Hinault in 1978, 1979, 1981, and 1982, and Fignon in 1983. Anybody could have managed Hinault to victory, but Van Impe, who left Gitane after his victory, had been a winner neither before nor since, and Fignon had been offered a professional contract by nobody except Guimard.

This success gave him the glow of a miracle man, but Guimard was simply a shrewd, hardworking official, innovative in a sport where tradition is strong. He had been no more than a middle-ranking professional rider himself, yet managed to win more than his share: seven stages in the Tour de France during the early 1970s, although he had never finished higher than seventh in the race; third place twice in the world championships; and the points jersey once in the Tour of Spain. This was the record of an overachiever. As a manager he had a winning reputation that attracted some of the best amateur riders—it's great to be young and a Renault—while the Peugeot team struggled to find good new riders although it had a manpower pool of nearly 5,000 amateurs through the teams it equipped. Guimard spent long hours studying the results of amateur races, explaining that he was not looking simply for winners. He liked to find riders with character, becoming more interested in LeMond when he threw his bicycle off the road in fury at losing and seeking out Jules as an amateur when everybody said he had too strong a temperament. "I said to myself, If nobody likes him, perhaps the kid isn't so bad." Guimard kept in close touch with officials of amateur teams and followed a rider even if he had turned professional with another team, occasionally signing one for Renault after his obligatory two-year contract had lapsed. Some teams shied away from neoprofessionals, choosing to sign tested riders, but Guimard had built his success on signing amateur riders and molding them to his system. For this he had his critics. Since economics and race opportunities fixed team rosters at fifteen to twenty men, when Guimard was negotiating with three amateurs, he was sending a signal to three of his veterans that they would not be back next season.

Guimard brushed this point aside and lost his veterans, frequently rebuilding his team. Of his ten men in the 1984 Tour de France, only one was older than twenty-six; most were twenty-four or less. He chose his men well, surrounding his two leaders with such riders as Pascal Poisson, who said simply, "I don't think I have the strength or temperament to be a leader, I know my limits." What Poisson hoped for, what he once described as "my dream," was to become "the sort of *équipier* who is capable of winning a big victory once in a while but who is above all a rider devoted to his leader." Or Marc Madiot, who could win in Louvroil and talk about his early reputation for clumsiness descending mountains, saying, "I was beginning to get a complex, but one person has taught me confidence and that's Cyrille Guimard. He didn't make fun of me or chew me out. He tried to understand, to explain things to me, to build me up." Responding, Guimard said, "I like to find boys like Madiot, who don't need to win to be satisfied, who will work for a leader but who could win someday." For Hinault, Guimard had become too difficult a man to deal with, an overstrict manager who refused to give an experienced rider enough freedom, but for the young team he brought to the Tour, Guimard was the teacher they felt they still needed. "The team spirit is super," Jules said in the spring. "I've never seen it so good."

The manager's pride was equally high. His team was young, it was strong, and it was French, a big factor in a country with a reputation for xenophobia and an immigrant-worker population of one in twelve. Guimard had never had many foreigners riding for Renault, and he seemed to sum up his feelings when he said exultantly one day, "We can almost be considered France's national team."

Where did that leave the struggling American, LeMond?

○

Late in the evening, after the riders had finished the 338 kilometers from Nantes to Bordeaux, Greg LeMond would describe this ninth stage as "boring," adding, "Like the plane flight to California, it went on forever." The road had been entirely flat and rather pretty, passing through fields of sunflowers, their huge heads drooping before they were cut down and pressed for their oil, and the first vineyards of the Bordeaux region, where the grapes were still hard and green under the July sun. In these villages of the Vendée Department, counterrevolution had stirred in the late eighteenth century and the battle cry had been, "If I advance, follow me; if I retreat, kill me; if I die, avenge me."

As more than one account noted afterward, the words might have been written for use by Bernard Hinault. Trailing Laurent Fignon in the overall standings by 1 minute 29 seconds, Hinault began looking for bonuses, attempting to gain handfuls of seconds by winning the bonus sprints sprinkled along the route. Just short of 30 minutes in time bonuses were distributed throughout the Tour, usually in the dull stretches, in hopes that the riders would enliven the race by contesting these three or four daily sprints. Hinault, Fignon, and Sean Kelly had dueled occasionally before for these bonuses, but mostly had left them to lesser riders; the general feeling was that contenders should not quarrel over crumbs. By going for the crumbs now—a total of 3 minutes was available today—Hinault showed his impatience and even a trace of desperation.

In the village of La Planche, he won the sprint, collecting the 12 seconds that would be deducted from his overall time and the 8 points that counted toward the green jersey. Jacques Hanegraaf of Kwantum was second, collecting 8 seconds and 5 points, and Kelly was third, collecting 4 seconds and 3 points. In Chauché, 27 kilometers farther on, Hinault did not figure in the sprint, although he was still riding at the front of the pack, fearing the mass crashes that usually started toward the middle of the pack. Under the hot sun on a long, listless course, the crash came at kilometer 74. The last to arise was Hinault's teammate Christian Jourdan, a journeyman *équipier*, grimacing in pain and clutching his right calf. As word passed up the pack that Jourdan had been left behind and was being treated by a Tour doctor, La Vie Claire sent Bernard Vallet back to find out how his teammate was doing. He returned without any certain information. A few minutes later Dominique Arnaud and Alain Vigneron drifted back, only to return without any news. Finally Hinault slowed and let the pack pass him. When he was at the rear, Jourdan appeared, pedaling slowly with his calf wrapped in a heavy white bandage. Hinault pulled alongside him and, as Jourdan put his right hand to his temple to hide his tears, threw his right arm around Jourdan's shoulders. Silently they rode on together for a minute before Hinault had to return to work. He pedaled up the road and wove through the pack toward the front, while Jourdan stopped and climbed into the ambulance, his race finished.

○

Just up the road, in the village of Saint-Jean-de-Beugne, at kilometer 94, with 244 kilometers to go, lay the third bonus sprint of the day. Hinault went over the line first, with Pascal Simon of the Peugeot team second and Hanegraaf third. Kelly was also sprinting hard, and as they passed the line, Hinault and Kelly looked back, saw a gap between their sprinting group and the rest, and took off. In the moment of panic, when the riders in front picked up the beat and those behind could not react, the Hinault group gained a lead of 30 seconds. Nobody could say the breakaway had been planned, and probably it hadn't, although La Vie Claire seemed to have a lot of riders in the sprint. Maurice Le Guilloux was there, and so were Charly Bérard, Vallet, and Arnaud, men with no reason to be at the front but ideal companions in a breakaway. Twenty-one riders were in on the break, and many of them were team leaders: Simon, Kelly, Kim Andersen and Michel Laurent of Coop, Jean-René Bernaudeau of Système U, and Paulo Ferreira of Sporting Lisbon. The rest were workmen: Jean-François Chaurin and Pierre Bazzo of Coop, Graham Jones of Système U, Jérome Simon of La Redoute, Ludo Peeters of Kwantum, Fédérico Echave of Teka, Glauco Santoni of Carrera-Inoxpran. Renault had only two men in the group,

Dominique Gaigne and Yvon Madiot. Fignon and LeMond had been trapped, left behind, expecting the sprinters to slow down once across the line. With them were two other team leaders, Stephen Roche of La Redoute and Joop Zoetemelk of Kwantum, who realized quickly what was happening and who tried to join the Hinault group.

The breakaway was going too fast by then, and Roche and Zoetemelk could not jump the gap. If only, if only . . . If they had, Renault would have been left with only Panasonic as a strong ally and Hinault would have been gone, eight teams pulling against two. "It could have been a thirty-minute break," Paul Sherwen of La Redoute judged. Instead, Hinault managed no better than a 35-second lead before Renault reorganized. Its riders fell into the formation of a team time trial, tugging everybody along. Panasonic had to follow, and so did La Redoute and Kwantum. Up went the pace to nearly 60 kilometers an hour. When a team is chasing over a flat road, it sees its opponents far ahead and what counts is that it makes progress, even slowly. As long as the distance is narrowing, the chasers have the psychological advantage. Renault had it now. Ahead the breeze shifted from the left—a good pusher—to a head wind. "When the wind changes like that, it makes a mess of you," Kelly said. With 240 kilometers to go and the mountains two days away, there was too much to lose fighting the head wind and not succeeding. Twenty kilometers after the trap was sprung, Hinault was overtaken. ("Audacity isn't always enough," he has admitted.)

Had the glass been half full or half empty? Had Hinault sent a message to Fignon or the other way around? Hinault had shown that he would attack anywhere, even at a mundane bonus sprint; Renault had shown its power to counterattack. The obvious lesson was the old one that only a strong team can afford to take the yellow jersey early. Few other teams could have protected the race leader by mounting Renault's pursuit. For men with weak teams, like Kelly and Hinault, this was something to think about as the pack settled down.

At the next bonus sprint, Kelly won and Hinault was second, with Renault vigilant. At the one after that, Fignon preceded Kelly and Hinault across the line. The bonus game was over, and the sprints ahead were left to lesser riders. For the day, Hinault gained 40 seconds, Kelly 24, and Fignon 12. Still looking for his first victory, Kelly had managed only fourth place behind the winner, Jan Raas of the Kwantum team. The long day was over, and late on a Saturday night in Bordeaux, with the wine flowing and a late start scheduled the next morning, everybody was talking about how dreary the stage would have been without Hinault's breakaway. Nine hours 40 minutes: as the French proverb said, As long as a day without bread. The bit of excitement reminded someone of the old joke about the man who went to his doctor for a routine examination and was told to stop drinking, smoking, and carousing. "If I do all that, will I live longer?" the patient asked. "I can't promise that," the doctor said, "but it will certainly seem longer."

○

Who's to say what Jan Raas told Marc Madiot as they swept down the Quai Louis XVIII toward the finish line at Bordeaux—or even if Raas told Madiot anything. Madiot had a clear lead and seemed headed for his second stage victory until Raas pulled even with him. Because Raas was the stronger sprinter and thus could be assured of the victory, Madiot might have accepted the inevitable. Or he might have been disposed to listen to even sweeter reason. In similar circumstances, Raas had a reputation for effective public speaking, for being able to slide up to a leader and explain things in such a way that allowed him to win races. He had long been a champion in the spring classics, a winner of Paris-Roubaix, many times a winner of the Amstel Gold Race, the reigning champion of the Netherlands, world champion in 1979. Sometimes there was a whiff of deceit about his victories: the world championship may or may not have involved assistance from a team car, perhaps a push, perhaps some shelter from the wind. Rumors of a payoff surrounded at least one victorious Amstel Gold Race.

When a rider is negotiating the outcome of a race, he can be either vague in his proposition—"You do something for our team now and we'll be sure to do something for yours later"—or he can quite specifically speak in sums. Folklore puts the ceiling in a big race at the equivalent of $1,000. Most riders are inclined to listen, because the personal favor, the team favor, and the bribe are part of the sport.

The ethical line is easily smudged, since everybody understands the team favor, the alliance that must be made for mutual benefit. As for a personal favor, the French call it sending back the elevator, and smile approvingly. About bribes there is less approval, but there is understanding that life is hard and that the riders are usually underpaid or embittered. Here is Raymond Martin just before his retirement in 1982: "It was in Paris-Bourges. I was ahead, one of the few times I was anything but an *équipier.* I sold out; I was wrong and I know it. But I thought of all the wrongs that had been done to me and it was a kind of revenge for me, a way of showing that I wasn't stupider than the rest. The races that I've sold since, it was only when I was out of it, burned up. You don't win often enough to give up a victory."

Whatever the proposition, Raas had the reputation of being listened to. He was a smart rider, a tough one, a throwback to the days when the riders might descend on a village café and top up their plastic water bottles with the local red wine. Nowadays nobody rides on wine, not even here in the Bordeaux country, with the road snaking past the esteemed Château Palmer. What riders drink now are tea laced with sugar, or mineral water, anything healthy and sensible. Raas was one of the few highwaymen left, road captain for Raleigh for years and now for Kwantum. In the spring he took a terrible spill in the Milan-San Remo race, hurtling off the course on a curve, and losing two months of his season recuperating. At age thirty-two, here he was again a winner in the Tour de France despite his lack of opportunities. A poor climber and a middling time trialist, he had again captured "my stage," the triumph that compensates so many riders for the rest of their ordeal. The victory in Bordeaux was his tenth since his debut in the Tour in 1977, far from Eddy Merckx's record of thirty-four. But then only eighteen men have ever won more than Raas, and only two of them, Hinault and Zoetemelk, were still riding. "I won my stage," the riders exult, and trudge on, satisfied. Listen to Aldo Donadello, whose moment of glory was a sixth place once in Italy's championship, tell why, riding for the Kas team in the Tour de France a few years back, he relayed not another obscure rider but a dangerous rival, Hennie Kuiper, a leader of the Raleigh team: "Kuiper said to me, 'If you help me, I'll do everything to let you win the stage.' A victory in the Tour, it's my dream. It's always been a dream of mine, a stage victory. I went for it. I almost succeeded. Too bad we were caught. My conscience is absolutely clear. What I did, others have done to me. I've had more tears than laughs in my career. I'm twenty-eight years old and you can imagine what a victory would have meant for me."

Among the riders Raas also inspired respect and even affection for his way with the rules—as in the Tour of Switzerland some years ago. "We had to sign a form before we started in the morning and a form when we finished in the evening. It was cold and raining and the official's pen never worked. After a few days of this, I got fed up and told the official that this was stupid and that all the riders wanted to do was take a shower and get out of their racing clothes. Of course this didn't change anything, so I took the form out of his hands, and while the other riders applauded, I tore that piece of paper into a thousand pieces. The result was that I was suspended for three years in Switzerland. But when I was able to ride there again, I found they weren't using the form anymore."

Raas tore up the rules and Raas made the rules. Barely noticed after his victory in Bordeaux was the absence of any Panasonic rider in the final duel. The closest Dutch rival was Eric Vanderaerden, fifth in the same time as 132 other riders, 5 seconds behind. It was not like Panasonic to let a Kwantum go unchased. In the tenth stage the next day, a 198-kilometer trip from Bordeaux to Pau through soldierly forests of turpentine pines, Vanderaerden registered Panasonic's first victory, winning a two-man breakaway from Marc Dierickx of Europ Décor. The pack was led in by Sean Kelly, 2 minutes 31 seconds behind, and the closest Kwantum rider was Leo Van Vliet, fourth in the same time as 136 other riders.

Just before the mountains, where neither team had much of a chance, the Dutchmen had reached a truce. At the bottom of it was, of course, Raas. "We could have won several stages, but the Panasonics were so quick to stop us that all they succeeded in doing was handing the victory over to a Belgian or a Frenchman on another team. And we did the same thing to them. After Jules' victory in Nantes, our team decided that this couldn't go on." During the trek to Bordeaux, Raas and Van Vliet of Kwantum had held a peace conference with Vanderaerden and Henk Lubberding of Panasonic. As they rode along, Raas, it can be assumed, did most of the talking.

*T*o *most people associated with the Tour*
de France, Greg LeMond was "the American," but to a sizable bloc he
was *el norteamericano*, the North American—accent on North. This
Spanish-speaking group comprised fifteen bicycle racers from Colombia, ten on its national amateur team and five with European professional teams. Shouting loud encouragement was a press corps of
forty radio, television, and newspaper reporters, providing what
seemed to be twenty-four-hour coverage to Colombia, where bicycling
is the national sport.

The distinction between *norte* and *sudamericanos* was important
to the Colombians, who wanted to be considered an international bicycling power with a distinct national identity. After all, they pointed
out, with due respect to LeMond, the world champion was the fellow
who had finished only thirty-first in that spring's major race in Colombia, the Clásico R.C.N. In the same race, Laurent Fignon finished
forty-third. The Colombians also noted that in 1980, Alfonso Florez, a
member of their team here, won the Tour de l'Avenir in France, a
showcase for young talent. Then in 1984, Martin Ramírez won the
Dauphiné Libéré, beating the esteemed Bernard Hinault in a decisive
time trial.

With this record, the Colombians had come to Europe the last two
years with dreams of becoming conquistadores, subduing the natives
with their firepower and potent magic. It hadn't happened that way.

When the Tour de France was first opened to amateur teams in
1983, the Colombians arrived amid great ballyhoo, although some riders, notably Hinault, pointed out that the geography of the course was
against them. Renowned climbers in the thin air of their homeland,
the Colombians did not reach the mountains in Europe until after ten

days of torture. First they had to ride over unfamiliar cobblestones, which battered them physically and psychologically as they lost great slices of time. A team time trial, a discipline strange to the Colombians, left them further behind. And the length of the daily stages broke them a bit more each day, especially when the weather turned brutally hot. They had no sense of tactics, people said, and they subsisted on coffee, which cost them sleepless nights.

The 1983 Tour ended with only five of the ten Colombians riding and their best finisher in sixteenth place. They had their moments in the mountains, but overall the visit was a fiasco. Things were going better in 1984, especially after the cobblestones were eliminated, the team trial shortened, and the length of the daily stages somewhat reduced. The average was near 200 kilometers, still higher than the 160 kilometers common in Colombia.

It hadn't been easy. "They warned me," said the star of the Colombian team, twenty-three-year-old Luis Herrera, "but I didn't believe the Tour could be so difficult. The last fifty kilometers of each stage are raced at a terribly swift pace. It's impossible to compare the Tour with our usual races. Here it's ten times tougher."

One reason was that in the thin air of home, Colombian riders develop a higher ratio of red blood cells than European riders have. These red blood cells carry more oxygen to their muscles, allowing them to outlast Europeans in the mountains, but the ratio begins to decrease after about a month down from altitude. LeMond was familiar with the phenomenon from the days when he rode in Colorado, and warned that the Colombians had brought their team over too soon for the Tour, that their extra days of training in Europe would work against them in a lowered number of red blood cells.

This theory was to be tested as the riders reached Pau, the jumping-off point into the Pyrenees, where the Colombians could begin to make things tougher for the other teams. It was about time, Colombian supporters said, because some European riders seemed to have gone out of their way to make things tough for the visitors in earlier races. More than once the Europeans had allowed, even encouraged, a breakaway by one of their own, regardless of European team rivalries, knowing that the Colombians would not pursue. The Colombians looked only for exploits, the general complaint ran, and were not willing to do the team's work that European racing demanded.

The Colombians came in for specific abuse, with Hinault leading the attack, mocking them as amateurs at 20,000 francs a month, the same criticism he has leveled at East European amateur riders. He went so far as to toy dangerously with Ramirez during the Dauphiné Libéré, swerving and braking unexpectedly with the Colombian close behind.

Thus far in the Tour everybody had been calmer, perhaps because the Colombians had not been a threat. The closest they had come was verbally warning that they would stick together and help one another, whether on the national team or on a European one. The policy was no different than the unity expected of the French, say, or the Belgians, no matter what team they might race for, but somehow it made people edgy about the Colombians' intentions.

Herrera was noncommittal about his team's strategy in the mountains and how quickly the Colombians would attack. The general feeling was that the Colombians hoped it would be tomorrow the Pyrenees, the day after tomorrow the world.

○

Or maybe the day after the day after tomorrow. Luis Herrera did finish second in the climb into the Pyrenees, but the easy winner was Robert Millar of Scotland—so easy a winner that with a kilometer to go in the eleventh stage, he had the time and presence of mind to take a Peugeot cap out of the pocket of his jersey and fit it snugly on his head. Why waste an opportunity for publicity for his team? Herrera was 41 seconds behind him, a long distance on the climb to the ski resort of Guzet-Neige.

Up here in the mountains it was steamy hot, but at the start of the day in Pau it had been foggy and cool, with the Pyrenees hidden until the sun burned the mist off the raw mountains. At the other end of these mountains between France and Spain, at Prades, Pablo Casals had celebrated Bach with the Brandenburg Concertos, and that is the music many people still hear in the Pyrenees, the joyous Bach, not the geometrician. At lunch a man from Marseille was complaining about the Pyrenees, however. "They have no business sense here," he said. "It's not like the Alps, with all their chalets and ski runs. Here it's all underdeveloped." He swung an arm toward the flinty mountains, covered only in trees. A long way off could be heard either a power saw or a small plane, but on the side of this mountain there was only the sound of crickets. "No business sense at all," repeated the man from Marseille, who was forced to live here because of his wife's job. He himself was retired, he said, and missed Marseille and its hustle and the Alps and the way the smallest village there worked to attract winter tourists. "Here you get only the crippled," he said, referring to Lourdes and its pilgrims farther along the road. The Tour went through Lourdes later in the afternoon, passing the many signs pointing to the sanctified grotto and the ranks of invalids sitting in wheelchairs at the curb. Lourdes is a recognizably French name, but the names of many other towns along the route were Basque sounds: Baudreix, Mirepeix, Igon, Arcizac, Pouzac, Avezac, Tuzaguet, Augirein, Orgibet, Aucazein, Seix, and Ercé.

The climb in the Pyrenees was minor compared to most years, with the day's major passes the Portet d'Aspet (1,069 meters high), the Col de la Core (1,375 meters high), and the finish at the summit of Guzet-Neige (1,480 meters high). The famous passes were missing—the Aubisque, the Tourmalet, the Aspin, the Peyresourde, "the Circle of Death"—those peaks that caused Henri Desgrange to be denounced as an assassin when the riders had first climbed them in 1910. Rumor said that the organizers chose a different route this year to avoid the possibility of a demonstration, even sabotage, by Spanish Basques eager for publicity. The day's peaks, the rumor went, were farther from the Spanish border and somehow easier to police. Another rumor had it that the classic route was dropped to keep the Colombians from an easy victory over a strenuous climb. As usual, the organizers did not explain. The Tour de France is Olympian, and where more suitably than in the mountains?

Tens of thousands of spectators were out for the day, perched mainly atop the peaks to watch through binoculars as the snaking column of riders moved through the valleys and up the roads slashed narrowly into the mountainsides. Slowly they came, trying to stay together. The trick in the mountains is to choose the man to beat and stay close to him, reckoning that if he does finish among the leaders, so will everybody marking him. Millar was a good rider to stay near, since he had won in the Pyrenees the year before, but this time he set too fast a pace for most of the others. In thirty-sixth place overall, 18 minutes 34 seconds behind, Millar seemed unlikely to finish so far ahead that he would take over the yellow jersey. A rider needed less time to make up, something like the 2 minutes 45 seconds that Pascal Simon overcame the year before when he finished third on the day and took the overall lead. That was a day of *la grande lessive,* the big housecleaning, and Simon took advantage of the Aspin and Tourmalet, leaving his two leaders, Phil Anderson and Stephen Roche, unprotected as he made his move. In trouble on the climb, Anderson yelled for Simon to stay and help him, but the Frenchman was listening only to inner voices. It was a classic case of betrayal by a support rider, but at the end of the day Simon was too important a rider to be bothered by such accusations from Anderson, now 9 minutes behind, or Roche, now 12 minutes behind. Their races were over and Simon's was just beginning. So it seemed, until he fell the next day and fractured his shoulder blade. At the end of the season Anderson moved to Panasonic and Roche to La Redoute, leaving Simon the unchallenged leader of the Peugeot team, a position greater than his talent. Nobody was marking Simon today. He began the Tour deliberately in middling shape, the old-fashioned way of riding into top physical condition during the first ten days, but the strategy had not worked; he neither grew stronger nor did the others wane.

As the sun stood overhead, the road tar began to soften, complicating the work of the riders as they descended from a summit to the next valley. Soft tar allows the flints and stones of the roadbed to work loose and puncture a tire, a bad thing on a climb, when the rider loses his rhythm and momentum, but a terrible thing on a descent, when the result is a high-speed crash. Descending is a special skill, and the best at it are virtual kamikazes, moving at speeds up to 80 kilometers an hour through sharp curves. The best descenders are nearly always fearless, and strong enough to brake deep into a turn, keeping control of their bicycle without losing much speed. In Paris-Nice, somebody remembered, Sean Kelly had said to an ace descender, his teammate Frédéric Vichot, "Take off and I'll follow and we'll open a gap." Vichot shot ahead, with Kelly on his wheel, and they opened a 30-meter lead on the pack. It went very well, with Vichot choosing the line of descent and Kelly simply following, until Kelly flew into a ditch because Vichot was going just too fast for anybody to stay on his wheel. The best descenders do anything for that extra bit of speed; Pedro Delgado, a Spaniard with the Reynolds team, had an especially terrifying position as he leaned far out over the handlebars to streamline his body and get his weight forward on the drop. Nobody else was willing to take the risk of being catapulted off the bicycle. Bernard Hinault, a strong descender, once experimented with guiding his bicycle with one hand and holding the other arm outstretched behind him, again for streamlining, but soon gave it up.

Coming down from the Col de la Core, Pierre Bazzo of the Coop team lost control and crashed, breaking no bones but tearing his left arm and hand. Bleeding heavily, he was put into an ambulance and sped to a hospital, one of ten riders who did not finish the day. Those who did were led by Millar, Herrera, and Delgado into the resort, empty during the summer, a collection of angular modern chalets with a lovely view of the valleys below where the chalets did not block it. The man from Marseille would have been pleased.

Most of the favorites stayed together, and it was not a day of *la grande lessive*. Greg LeMond struggled badly, far behind in the climb at the first pass, the Portet d'Aspet. He fought back on the descent and managed to finish sixteenth, 3 minutes 42 seconds behind Millar, gathering praise from his team officials. "If he wins the Tour, it's because of that stage," said one. "What he did was extraordinary. He has an iron will." Cyrille Guimard agreed, saying, "Greg had a great day." Sometimes the absence of total defeat is a victory.

Renault was full of congratulations. To general astonishment, Vincent Barteau finished nineteenth, 4 minutes 10 seconds behind, and kept the yellow jersey. He seemed safe as the overall leader for another week, until the next mountains, the Alps. One question had been answered: Paulo Ferreira was not, after all, a climber. The Portuguese finished dead last, 59 minutes 43 seconds behind.

But Laurent Fignon had scored again off Bernard Hinault. On the final approach to the finish, Fignon began to think that Hinault was in trouble. "I watched him and realized he wasn't having a very good day," Fignon said. "I told Guimard I would attack five kilometers from the end. He told me not to, and I waited." Guimard explained that Hinault could still rally with 5 kilometers left, but that at a shorter distance, time would run out. "At three kilometers I took off," Fignon said. He picked up 52 seconds on Hinault, just enough to have made a point. "You don't lose the war because you lose a battle," Hinault retorted. "There's still two long weeks to go and anything can happen."

○

Long ago, but only a year earlier, Joop Zoetemelk, a Dutchman, could never be written about in a French newspaper without being identified sooner or later in the story as Honorary Frenchman No. 1. He had earned this heartfelt title during the 1970s while he was riding and winning for French teams. His marriage to a Frenchwoman, with whom he opened a hotel in Meaux, near Paris, only added to his status.

His strong-willed wife ran the hotel because, as everybody said, Zoetemelk cared only about cycling and had a head for nothing else. This seriousness was celebrated. Every winter was devoted to training —daily jogging or cross-country cycling and skiing. "I can't stand inactivity," Zoetemelk liked to say. His form was so far ahead of other riders' that he excelled in spring races; he hated cold and rain, and so concentrated on races in the south of France. In 1980 he joined the Raleigh team in the Netherlands but returned to France after a year, saying, "I quit mostly because I couldn't face starting the season in Belgium with the rain, the cold, the cobblestones. At my age, what I want are some nice little races in France, the Tour du Tarn or Tour de l'Aude, the Midi Libre, where I can get ready for the season peacefully."

Zoetemelk never seemed to care about the grand exploit, and his career was studded with triumphs in nice little races. He won the somewhat negligible Tour du Haut-Var three times and would have won a fourth time except that he had the bad luck to be misdirected down a side street near the finish and could not make up the lost time when he realized his mistake. His first victory in the Haut-Var came in 1973; his last, in 1983.

By then, Zoetemelk was often held up as an example to younger riders because he was thirty-six years old. Thus, according to Raymond Poulidor, his captain in the early 1970s: "Joop is, above all, a serious rider. He trains like a youngster no matter what the weather." Or Louis Caput, another old-timer: "Joop proves that the modern theory that a rider is over the hill at thirty is false. When a champion declines it's because he no longer has the willpower to make the sacrifices that his job demands. He can still do it physically, but not in his heart."

Zoetemelk's attitude fit in well with the message that teams were sending their riders in the early 1980s. "Under the present economic conditions, everyone should realize that it's more and more difficult to find the money to keep a team going," said the manager of his Coop team, Jean-Pierre Danguillaume. "Zoetemelk has understood this. He couldn't set a finer example."

He could be courageous as well. In 1974, after a crash in the Midi Libre, a spinal infection nearly killed him. When he recovered, it was assumed he would stop riding, but he was back the next season, although his doctors said it would take him five years to regain his full strength.

In addition to his devotion to his work, Zoetemelk was celebrated for his caution. When he first became a professional in 1970, he was the butt of a joke that went, "Why is Zoetemelk always so pale?" The answer was "Because he always rides in Merckx's shadow"—a reference to Merckx's charge that Zoetemelk was that most despised of riders, a wheel-sucker, the man who lets somebody else do the work and keeps his strength to zip by at the finish. Zoetemelk denied the charge, which died out. If he ever was a wheel-sucker, it must have been out of caution or timidity; nearly 7 minutes ahead with one stage to go in the 1980 Tour de France, he could still say publicly, "Nothing is won yet, nothing can be won until we cross the finish line." Worse, he probably believed this.

Not often did Zoetemelk exceed himself. Bridging the Merckx and Hinault eras, he finished second in the Tour de France a record six times, in 1970, 1971, 1976, 1978, 1979, and 1982. He won just once, in 1980, when Hinault, leading at the halfway point, had to withdraw because of the initial attack of tendinitis in his right knee. The Dutchman's first bad year followed the Tour victory, and people began to wonder if Zoetemelk had grown too old. "Father Joop," Hinault had long called him, and not out of affection.

But Zoetemelk recovered in 1982, and then explained that the problem was that he had neglected his training during the previous winter.

"What killed me was all the demands on my time during the winter. You know me, I like it quiet, and all those receptions, banquets, and personal appearances just wiped me out. By the time they were all over, I just wanted to stay at home, and so I neglected my training." No more mistakes: back he went to the jogging, cross-country cycling and skiing, the winter training, the spring victories, the season designed to march in small steps toward the Tour de France.

Nobody ever accused Zoetemelk of bravado or panache. Asked in 1982, when things were going well for him again, if he thought he could win the Tour, he replied honestly, "No, there's no point dreaming. Finishing in the top five would be satisfying and a place on the podium more than honorable." He knew and accepted his limits, which could also be his strengths. "What knocks me out is Zoetemelk's intelligence in a race," said Luis Ocaña, the winner of the 1973 Tour. "He always works within his means, he decides on a goal and usually achieves it. Often it's second or third place, and that's just where he'll finish. He prefers not to throw himself into a decisive battle, but to fight his way slowly up the ladder. That's just the way he is."

Riding for Coop in the 1983 Tour de France, with Hinault sidelined, Zoetemelk was rated among a small group of favorites. When Coop scored an unexpected victory in the team time trial in the second stage, Kim Andersen took the yellow jersey, and Zoetemelk, second by a few seconds, seemed well-placed with attention focused on his teammate. But it became obvious after a few days that something was wrong. Zoetemelk was riding badly and seemed mournful. Soon it was announced that he had failed the drug test after the team time trial. His appeal had also failed. All this was known to him, but he had not said a word publicly. What would people think?

As riders usually do, Zoetemelk denied taking illegal drugs and insisted the urine test had been wrong. Obviously demoralized, he finished the Tour twenty-third overall, 47 minutes behind. Everybody expected him to end his protests, go home, and probably retire. He'd had a long and moderately glorious career—and, besides, who really cares about a doping charge?

For once, second place was not enough for Zoetemelk. Reversing his long habit of taking small steps, he startled the bicycling world by bringing a court suit to clear his name. Riders had protested before and some had written letters to the authorities, but few had sought legal redress. Zoetemelk was strongly supported by his wife and by the Dutch cycling federation, but the name on the court suit was his. He sued the Tour organizers and was rebuffed legally. The case went from court to court, with medical experts offering contradictory findings.

Zoetemelk insisted that his body naturally produced an excess of hormones, which showed up in the urine test. More experts and counteropinions were needed, and then it was spring, with the case still not settled, and Zoetemelk had switched from the French Coop team to the new Kwantum team in the Netherlands. Now, in newspaper articles, he was no longer Honorary Frenchman No. 1 but the Dutchman, sometimes the thirty-seven-year-old Dutchman. Why did so many reporters seem embarrassed to see Zoetemelk militant?

Interviewed in the spring of 1984, he was asked why exactly he was still racing. He replied, "I get asked that a lot . . . Since last year, I've been thinking only of the Tour, where I was the victim of an enormous injustice. It's become an obsession and I won't have any peace until the race."

No happy endings: This was his Tour too many. He never had liked racing in the Pyrenees, in contrast to good placings in the Alps, and the eleventh stage from Pau was a disaster. Long after the main pack finished, while motorists fretted because the road was still closed to traffic to protect the stragglers, an ashen Zoetemelk rode in 19 minutes behind the winners. "It's all over for me," he said when he found his breath. "This is my last Tour." Starting the day eighteenth overall, a bit more than 4 minutes behind Fignon, he fell to sixty-fourth place.

A few days later he confirmed the decision. "I'll finish my contract with Kwantum at the end of the year and stop racing," he said placidly. "It's become too tough. No more Tours."

Zoetemelk would make it to Paris, as he always did, finishing for the fourteenth time in fourteen Tours. He ranked thirtieth, 1 hour 6 minutes 2 seconds behind, and then went home to spend his winter awaiting the court ruling. It still had not come by spring, when he was racing again for Kwantum but insisting that his days with the Tour de France were finished.

*T**here was no stopping Renault's riders as* the Tour made its way toward and through the Massif Central, the country's mountainous heartland and the transition between the Alps and the Pyrenees. Pascal Poisson, a support rider, surprised the sprinters to win the twelfth stage, from Saint-Girons to Blagnac, and Pierre-Henri Menthéour, rated No. 7 or 8 on the team, was first after a three-man breakaway on the thirteenth stage from Blagnac to Rodez. As Renault scored its sixth victory in thirteen stages, kept Vincent Barteau in the yellow jersey, and had Laurent Fignon fresh and strong behind him, *L'Equipe* described the team in a banner headline as "The New Cannibals."

These words stirred the original cannibal, Eddy Merckx, who was keeping himself far from the race even though he was technically a sponsor because his factory supplied bicycles for the Europ Décor team. From Belgium or Colorado or the Côte d'Azur, wherever he seemed to be while the Tour continued, Merckx issued his judgment: Fignon, Hinault, and Barteau, in that order, on the victory podium in Paris on July 22.

Having spoken, Merckx for once spoke no more. In his retirement, he had become that most dreaded of athletes, the one who always remembered how much better it was in his day, when ships were wooden and men iron, not vice versa, the way it was now. His quarrel with Fignon over training habits and dedication had been loud and public, and more than a few people in the bicycling world were delighted when Fignon dismissed Merckx as an old bore. When Francesco Moser of Italy broke Merckx's record for the hour's race against the clock in Mexico City earlier that spring, the Belgian had quickly protested that Moser had the advantage of improved technology and suggested that the record be disallowed, or at least have an asterisk attached to it. By the time the guffaws subsided, Merckx was joining in the congratulations to Moser, but too late. Tiring of his memories about how it had been in his golden age a decade before, reporters rarely sought Merckx out, so this year he was staying away, unloved.

○

It was different once—at the start of the 1977 Tour de France in Fleurance, for example. The applause began as Willy Teirlinck, an obscure rider for a Belgian team, moved onto the starting ramp in the prologue. At first Teirlinck seemed surprised and then diffident, but as the cheering grew louder, he looked up over his handlebars with a big grin. Only when some of the hundreds of people near the ramp started to chant "Eddy, Eddy" did Teirlinck realize that Merckx had appeared nearby. His smile gone, he ducked his head to concentrate on the clock marking the seconds until his start.

Surrounded by well-wishers, Merckx was, as usual, impassive. When he mounted the starting ramp, the crowd pressed in, the cheers grew louder, the cameramen swarmed around, and fathers lifted their small children for a look at Merckx in his final Tour. Even he said it would be his last. Of the six he had entered, he had won five, tying the record of Jacques Anquetil. But the last victory had been in 1974, when he was twenty-nine years old, healthy and strong. Now he was none of these.

At thirty he simply turned old. He was holding a 58-second overall lead in the 1975 Tour when his troubles began on an Alpine descent. The drop had been rapid and perilous, and, as sometimes happens, a delayed state of shock seemed to have set in. Merckx got the wobbles and could only struggle to the finish, losing his lead. Falling two days later and breaking his jaw, he soldiered on to finish second, but his championship days were over. By then, in a professional career dating to 1965, Merckx had won 400 races, including all the spring classics, five Tours de France, five Tours of Italy, and three world championships, but after the age of thirty he won only one big race, Milan-San Remo. Whatever it was that he lost on the mountain descent remained lost. He did not enter the 1976 Tour de France because of illness, and in 1977 he had entered few races.

Still he was emphatic about his chances in Fleurance. "If I no

longer believed I could win the Tour, I would no longer participate,"
he said. His reputation stayed with him. "Perhaps he is no longer the
great Merckx, but his name is still Merckx," said Lucien Van Impe,
who had won the Tour in 1976. In proof, Merckx pushed himself to
finish third in the 5-kilometer prologue. The next morning he seemed
relaxed and even confident, chatting, smiling, and signing autographs.
"I believe in victory," he said. "That helps me to accept the fact that
a day comes when the strength of youth declines. It's in the nature of
things and one submits to it even while still fighting to reach the limit.
It's in vain to say, 'With a little more rest, things would have worked
out better.' No, one has to continue, whatever the cost, and I have
continued. One has to know how to suffer."

He did suffer, especially in the Alps. By the time the race reached
Chamonix, he collapsed. Officially food poisoning was blamed, fooling
nobody who had watched Merckx roll his head from side to side and
gasp for breath during the climb into Chamonix. After an hour's treatment in the medical trailer, Merckx was able to continue, laboring
through the rest of the Alps and finally finishing sixth overall in Paris.

The next year, when the Tour started in Leiden, the Netherlands,
there was an Eddy Merckx team riding Eddy Merckx bicycles. All
along the route into Belgium salesmen offered a biography of Merckx
in comic strips and Merckx ceramic plates commemorating his splendid victories. Every sign of Eddy Merckx was present, but the race
began without him. He was supposed to have been a technical consul-
tant to the C&A team, one he helped assemble earlier that year while
he was still talking about a comeback, one last chance to win a record
sixth Tour. Merckx lived for records and for victories, racing an ex-
traordinarily heavy schedule during his vintage years, surrounded by
selfless *équipiers* whose only ambition was his. He had been with the
team for the prologue in Leiden, riding in a car behind the bicyclists,
looking anguished and despondent. Members of the Belgian team
seemed embarrassed to have his absence noticed. Joseph Bruyère,
Merckx's lieutenant for many years, looked down at his feet and said
only, "I haven't seen him today. Perhaps he's not here." A faraway look
came into the face of another rider, Walter Planckaert, when he was
pressed on whether Merckx was expected. "I don't know," he said.
"That's all. I don't know." Other C&A riders refused to discuss his

absence. Everybody, it seemed, was feeling bad about Merckx, though perhaps none as much as Merckx himself. All spring he had resisted suggestions that he should retire. He had entered no races—"Another victory, more or less, is meaningless," he insisted—and then had grudgingly announced that he was through as a rider. He became a team official and rode in a support car in one spring race; the photographs showed him standing through the open top of the C&A car, framed by bicycles lashed to the roof upside down.

That morning in Leiden in 1977, Raymond Poulidor, a rider in fourteen Tours de France, was walking around, cheery and buoyant, in the second year of his retirement. Poulidor was gracious, but then he never did win the Tour de France. The man who did, five times, and so badly wanted a sixth, was nowhere to be found.

○

Fons De Wolf looked in the mirror that morning in Rodez and saw staring back at him something he had never seen before. "I saw a monster," he boasted later. "And that monster was me." *King Kong.* Two days after he had announced in a Belgian newspaper that, at age twenty-eight, he finally had to admit he would never be a big winner, would always be a small man in the pack, De Wolf took one more look into the mirror. The monster gazed back, full of the certainty of victory today.

In the Place d'Armes, while the other riders were stuffing their jerseys with fruit and signing in for the fourteenth stage, a 227-kilometer run to the Domaine du Rouret, De Wolf was positively radiant. He glowed with strength and purpose, and nobody noticed. But then nobody had been noticing Fons De Wolf for some time.

When he turned professional in 1979, he was one of the first Belgians to be acclaimed the new Eddy Merckx, the winner of amateur titles in the Belgian championship and Paris-Roubaix. Darkly handsome and graceful, even elegant, *le beau Fons* became the darling of the fans. So much was expected of him that he had to fail, winning not much more than the points jersey in the 1979 Tour of Spain and the Tour of Lombardy the following year. Each year brought its success— Milan-San Remo in 1981, the Het Volk the year after—but after four years he had accumulated a record Merckx would compile in only one spring. By then De Wolf had left home and begun riding for an Italian team, far from the pressures in Belgium. His performance was steady: every spring he would win a classic, raise hopes that finally he had matured, and then nothing for the rest of the season. The Italians were indifferent when he returned to a Belgian team.

Along the way he had acquired a reputation as a playboy, which usually means the rider is as interested in the company of women as is any other yeasty, unattached male in his twenties. This is frowned on in the world of professional bicycling. "I've done some dumb things," the rider Pierre-Henri Menthéour admitted during the Tour a few years ago. "I like to go out, to sleep late. I like girls. I'm twenty-two years old and it's normal, isn't it? But the Paris-Nice race taught me a lesson. Before the start I spent a week with a girl without leaving the bedroom. The result was that I had a dreadful race, way behind, and even developed tendinitis, which took a month to heal. I realized there had to be a better way to get ready for a race. Cycling is a pretty decent way of life if you take it seriously. So now I do: I go to bed early and alone." To which answered Jacques Anquetil, the voice of the establishment: "Girls are something you shouldn't overdo because they don't do your legs any good. As with anything else, you need moderation. While Menthéour, De Wolf, and Michaud were collecting conquests, you didn't see them often on the winner's podium."

By 1984 De Wolf was nothing more than the first of the new Eddy Merckxes, none of whom were. And now, twice in one week he had heard bad news. First came the announcement that his Europ Décor team had done so badly all year that it would be disbanded or, at best, downgraded out of international competition the following year. There would be no place for De Wolf. Next, he was told that he had not been selected for the Belgian team that would compete in the world championship a month after the Tour de France. He could survive the breakup of his team by finding another, in Italy again or in Spain, but not to have been chosen for the World's was indeed a slap in the face. It meant that he was no longer rated among the ten best Belgian riders, even in a time of national bicycling decline. Nobody believed any longer in Fons De Wolf, who smiled at friends among the other riders, knowing a secret—the monster he had seen in the mirror. *King Kong.* To them he was ranked merely fifty-third in the overall standings, 29 minutes 34 seconds behind.

Luckily for De Wolf, no climber, there was no real climbing ahead but a series of gorges and sharp descents ending in a long slide down the mountain into yet another resort town eager for publicity, the Domaine du Rouret. Again it was time for the kamikaze descenders, the riders with the strength and nerve to ignore a sudden change from sunlight into a thickly shadowed plunge lined with trees and boulders waiting for a miscalculation. In the lunar landscape of the gorges, the place to be was at the front, where there was room to maneuver, and to stay there a rider had to keep moving. The road was bumpy as well as narrow. Back in the pack the riders were forced by sheer number and closeness to take the road's turnings at bad angles and too high a speed. If not particularly steep, the climbs were long and stressful. Combined with the bold descents, they were taking a toll on nerves. The riders had to weave between cars that were rushing ahead to fix a flat or that were crowded with reporters seeking a view of the race, and sometimes a rider would become so incensed at the obstruction that he would pound the hood of a car getting in his way.

Taking advantage of the terrain, two riders attempted breakaways, hoping to get over a hill and find a long and speedy drop. Nine others, including De Wolf, went after them and ran them down after 30 kilometers. Everybody was swallowed into the pack except De Wolf, still seeing his monster.

Nobody misunderstood him. When De Wolf was only 30 seconds ahead, Cyrille Guimard turned to a guest in his team car and announced, "This is a race he ought to win." And nobody cared if De Wolf did win. To them he was still *le beau Fons,* pretty boy Fons, nearly half an hour down, having his fun. Let him have it, more than one rider thought, tomorrow we'll have ours with him. Guimard had other things to worry about. Weaving his car through the pack, he pulled alongside Laurent Fignon and barked, "Get your head back in the race. People will attack soon." Five minutes later they did, but Fignon had been alerted. Attack and counterattack, climb and descend, and far up ahead De Wolf was ignored during one of the great rides of his life. It all seemed so easy as he put time and distance between himself and the others—25 minutes ahead by kilometer 196. He was not thinking, he said later, about the snub over the world championship or about the possibility that the Europ Décor team would be disbanded. What he thought, he said, was how strong he was, how fast, how invincible.

From time to time among the gorges the pack dropped its speed, allowing the laggards to catch up and escape possible disqualification for finishing too far behind. In the last 30 kilometers, Renault forced the speed back up and reduced De Wolf's final lead to 17 minutes 40 seconds, good enough to jump him from fifty-seventh to fourth in the overall standings. The first person he saw when he crossed the finish line was the same Belgian reporter to whom he had admitted two days earlier that he now knew and accepted his limits as just another rider. DE WOLF—C'EST FINI, the headline had run earlier in the week, a lifetime ago. *Fini?* Where do the writers get their information?

"Anything is possible," De Wolf shouted at the reporter. "I won today and I'll win again. This is just the beginning." *King Kong.*

"All he has to learn is how to suffer and he'll be one of the great riders," Anquetil said later. Early in De Wolf's career, Anquetil had touted him as a coming star, a possible winner of the Tour, until he soured and labeled him a playboy. Now here was cause for hope, a bit past the time when De Wolf could be considered the new Eddy Merckx and yet . . . *The new Eddy Merckx.*

The very next day De Wolf finished 121st, nearly 24 minutes behind, and fell back to 54th place, never to rise higher. *Le beau Fons.*

○

The riders in the Women's Tour were uneasy in the village of La Chapelle-en-Vercors, glancing nervously down the road where it lifted toward the Côte de Chalimont, 1,350 meters high and the first mountain they had to climb since their race had left Paris. "We're used to hills, so we're treating it like a hill, a very long hill," said Senta Bauermeister of the Canadian team. Jolanta Goral of the American team admitted, "We're not exactly intimidated. At least the rest of the team isn't, but I sort of am. I just don't know what it will be like." Only the two French teams were familiar with the Alps.

As they poured bottles of water over their heads to prepare for the hot ride ahead on their twelfth stage, many of the women were complaining. "I just can't climb," said Betsy King of the American team. "People I ride rings around are beating me on climbs." She said she had been weakened by medicine she was taking to relieve tendinitis.

Marianne Martin of the American team was also unhappy. "Some fun," she snorted. "We eat, drive, race, eat, drive, sleep." At least they were winning a measure of respect, as measured by Jacques Anquetil's newspaper column. When a reader wrote in to ask whether the women weren't riding basically because of the sexual sensation of being on a saddle, Anquetil had had his consciousness heightened enough to point out that, whatever the sensation, men shared it on a bicycle. He added, "I don't think that with the suffering the women have endured in the mountains, they've had the leisure to enjoy the pleasure of contact with the saddle." The longest journey, Chairman Mao said, begins with a single step.

Time to race. Down the road the thirty-six women went on a slight coast, the grayish stone of the mountain looming on the right across fields where cows grazed. The road took a sharp right and began moving up the mountain between long lines of spectators. Heleen Hage of the Netherlands, the yellow jersey, and Martin went quickly to the front as other riders began dropping back. Once left behind, they had to make their way alone, since each team in the women's race had only one support car, not two as the men's teams had. Nor were there the technical-support cars and ambulances the men could rely on for help. On this long climb and descent to Grenoble, only the leaders were supported. With barely 10 minutes gone, Henneke Lieverse of the Dutch team was abandoned as she fell behind; as it pulled to her level, her car slowed and a hand emptied a water bottle over her head. Then the car passed and was gone.

By kilometer 13 the pack had separated into two groups, fourteen women up ahead and the straggling rest. Because there were so few support cars, team managers tried to look out for all the riders, not simply their own. When the U.S. car passed Louise Garbutt of the British team, she got her dose of water. Struggling, looking almost disbelieving, Jolanta Goral was left behind. "How far to the top?" a French rider gasped at the Canadian car. "Not far, not far," said the driver and team manager, Michel Banos, deliberately vague. He sped up the narrow road, startling spectators as he wove through the bicycles. *"Douche, douche,"* called Hilary Matte of Canada, pleading for water to be poured over her. The car slowed and she got her shower; she then lowered her head and plugged onward. Banos left her behind, seeking the only Canadian at the front, Marilyn Wells, No. 6.

Kilometer 20: "You're doing fine, just fine," Banos shouted at Wells. "Breathe, breathe," he ordered. "You want some water? Take some water on your face." He pulled alongside and water was poured over Wells.

Kilometer 25: "Come on, Marilyn, to the front, come on." Banos thumped the roof of the car. "Just one minute fifty and you're at the front." He shouted encouragement to a French rider, Valérie Simmonet, one of the favorites before the race began but now trailing badly. "Come on, Valérie, *allez*."

Kilometer 27: "Catch the wheel, Marilyn, get up there, pass these two, get up with the leaders." Wells passed the two. The road began to drop and she was over the top, racing at 60 kilometers an hour down a wider road with gentle curves.

Kilometer 32: "Marilyn, breathe deeply, we have a minute thirty ahead to make up. Relax and now go." Obediently Wells went. For her reward she began overtaking riders, first Rita Timpers of the Dutch team and then Corinne Lutz of the French. The three of them rode together, relaying, as the road began to climb again.

Kilometer 35: "Come on, Marilyn, five girls in front, five girls."

Kilometer 38: Moving well, Simmonet and Deborah Shumway of the American team overtook Lutz, Timpers, and Wells. The car's race radio announced that the five were 50 seconds ahead of the next group and 53 seconds behind the leaders. The French A team's car pulled alongside and the manager, Yves Plaisance, shouted across to Banos, "You said rolling?" The speedometer showed 50 kilometers an hour, as good a speed as the men would reach when they passed later in the day.

Kilometer 42: "Work with the French, Marilyn, not the Dutch, the Dutch won't work. Go for it—you have a minute on four girls behind. Get the wheel, come on, Valérie, catch the wheel." Banos was urging a relay on Simmonet, but he had different advice for his own rider. "Don't let them catch your wheel," he ordered. "Come on, later on you'll relax." The road had narrowed again and the car sped along what passed for a shoulder, tearing out clumps of weeds with the fender.

Kilometer 46: Wells was working hard, but the leaders had opened their gap to 2 minutes 25 seconds. Banos thought it better to keep this secret. "They're just there," he said, giving nothing away. "Breathe deep, take air in your lungs. Come on, girl, watch the descent, stick on the wheel, you're losing too much time. Come on, girl." Wells nodded agreement.

Kilometer 47: The French A car pulled alongside again and Plaisance asked, "Can you cover for me for five minutes?" He wanted to fall back and look after some of his other riders. Banos agreed.

Kilometer 48: Pulling alongside Wells, Simmonet, and Shumway, Banos and a helper began spraying water on them. As it poured down her face, Simmonet opened her mouth to swallow it. "Thank you, thank you," Wells said. Shumway began screaming, "Cut it out, I can't see, cut it out."

Kilometer 49: The three closed to 1 minute 15 seconds on all the leaders except Marianne Martin, who was 2 minutes 45 seconds up. The radio had been wrong in saying all the leaders were together.

Kilometer 50: Banos considered dropping back to give water and encouragement to the other Canadian riders but decided not to. "She's all we've got for the victory," he said, nodding at Wells. The last climb was behind, and the long descent into Grenoble approaching. If Banos dropped back now, he would be unable to drive fast enough safely to find Wells again. As Grenoble became visible 20 kilometers away in the valley to the right, Simmonet, Shumway, and Wells joined up with all the leaders except Martin, settling Banos' decision.

Kilometer 58: The car was groaning on its suspension system as Banos fought to stay with Wells through hairpin curves. He could not get close enough to talk to her until Wells and Lutz began falling back, the distance between them and the leaders opening with each turn.

Kilometer 64: "Come on, Marilyn, 20 seconds, come on." Almost talking to himself, Banos explained why Wells had no chance to win. "Her problem is fear, and why not?" The speedometer showed 60 kilometers an hour. "Plus technical flaws, like going too wide on the turns. She's a good girl, rode a nice race."

Kilometer 69: "Don't push too big, only three kilometers to go. Not so far now, Marilyn." Wells signaled to Lutz that she should relay her, but Lutz shook her head in refusal. "Let her come up to you with seven hundred meters to go so you can get her," Banos yelled. The day's race had come down to a battle for seventh place.

Kilometer 71: "Change the gear now, push hard, stand up, stand up. That's it, super." Banos sprayed Wells with water. "The last two kilometers, push hard. We're getting into town, no more wind now."

Kilometer 72: "Just three hundred meters to go. Bigger gear now. Go, girl, go." Wells shifted gears, stood up on the pedals, and accelerated, beating Lutz by 10 seconds. She leaned her bicycle against a railing and sat down on the curb, unable to speak and having nothing to say.

On the victory podium above Wells' head, Martin looked remarkably fresh as she accepted the winner's bouquet. She had finished 1 minute 33 seconds ahead of Hage and reduced her overall lead to 1 minute 44 seconds. "I just love to climb," Martin said. "It was a beautiful ride, not as tough as I thought it would be." For Bauermeister, who tried to talk herself into believing the Alps were just a long hill, it was enough that she finished. "I survived," she said, once she caught her breath. "That's enough for one day."

E L E V E N

L*ike so many American women, Anne* Anderson enjoys visiting her husband at work now and then, "just to understand better what he does and how he does it," as she puts it. But her husband, Phil Anderson, rides bicycles for a living, and Anne Anderson finds she is most unwelcome when she pays a call, especially during the Tour de France. "It's really a man's world," she said. "They just want women to stay home and have babies."

Anne Anderson was not easily kept at home, now the town of Waregem in Belgium. "She's a very determined woman" explained her father, Steve Robel, who has taught mechanical engineering at Seattle University for the last thirty-five years. "Anne will take any kind of challenge. She loves the excitement of it."

So she was happy to accept the challenge of being a woman in an overwhelmingly male environment. In 1983, on the Tour's day off, she, her father, her mother, Helen, and her brother, Chris, were out scouting the next day's route from L'Alpe-d'Huez to Morzine, looking for the best spots to stand and douse her husband with water during his ride through the sweltering Alps. By then the family were old hands at this. "During the time trial at Puy-de-Dôme, we all went out with the bottles of water and threw them at Philip," Anne Anderson recalled. "I missed, Dad missed, Chris missed, but Mom got him. Philip says he appreciates it."

Anderson, a twenty-six-year-old Australian who rides for the Panasonic team, was fourth overall in the standings when the 1984 Tour reached Grenoble, despite a bad crash on the descent. The year before he had finished ninth, and the year before that, fifth, and wore the leader's yellow jersey for ten days in the early going.

He always seemed to have trouble at L'Alpe-d'Huez, and during the long climb Anne did her best to encourage him. "About three kilometers from the finish, Anne was standing by the road, waiting for me," Anderson said of the 1983 race. "She ran alongside me and kept saying, 'You're going fine, it's almost over, go for it, I love you'—things like that. She also gave me water. I appreciated all of that."

"I like looking after my husband," Anne Anderson said. "I think what I do is reflected in his success." That is not the attitude of bicycling officials and team managers toward wives. "To put it mildly," she said, "they don't appreciate my presence. They think I'm distracting him." She denied that she was—or could. "I've had dinner with Philip once. My family and I also had a drink with him in his room once. That's it, that's all. Even if we wanted to spend a night together, Philip wouldn't do it because the team officials would disapprove."

The riders do feel that hearth and home can be distractions. Jean-Luc Vandenbroucke of La Redoute singled out his fellow Belgians: "The Belgians get bored in the Tour because it's too long and they're away from home too long. It's not true in my case because I've always raced for a French team, with all that moving around. In Belgium, where the races take place fifty kilometers from home, where you go home every night, you get accustomed to being a homebody." One year the Tour stopped for the night in Mouscron, where he lived in Belgium.

"I went home to change my laundry and kiss the kids, but I slept at the hotel with the team. I'm used to that kind of life."

Behind the official hostility is the conviction that sex harms an athlete during competition. The small world of the Tour was abuzz one year with the story of a wife who spent the night with her husband just before a time trial. He finished far below expectations, and the wife was asked to go home. With her gone, he finished the next major climb in far better time, "which only goes to prove that the theory about no sex is correct," as people kept saying.

Anne Anderson did not discuss the theory, but did not like what it said about women. "It's as if women are just here to play, not for business," she said. "They think that sex is something you don't do for six weeks before the Tour or any other race. It was much easier when Philip was in the yellow jersey. They'd do anything to keep him happy. Maybe they even thought I was doing something right since he was in the yellow jersey."

Among the ways she found to see her husband in the 1982 Tour was to pretend to be a reporter and follow him for a day in a press car. "I just wanted to have the experience of following my husband in the race," she explained. "So I disguised myself as a guy, wore a baseball hat and a jacket, stuffed my hair up in my hat, and went along."

The next year she had press credentials, since she was writing for a bicycling magazine in her hometown of Seattle. She graduated from Seattle University with a degree in art in 1977 and, after a six-month bicycling trip around Europe, returned home to attend the University of Washington to study medical illustrating. She met Anderson in 1978, when they both competed in the Red Zinger race in Colorado, the forerunner of the Coors Classic. After that race, Anderson went on to Edmonton, Alberta, where he won a gold medal in the Commonwealth Games, and she went back to Seattle. He began writing to her and they got together in 1979 at the Colorado race again. "He was racing, but I was just a spectator," she said. "Then we spent a few weeks together, and in 1980 he asked me to come over to Paris, where he was riding for an amateur team. I went and stayed awhile, and then we went back to the United States to introduce him to my folks. Then we went to Australia to see his folks and get married."

She expected that when her husband's bicycling days were over, they would move to the United States or Australia.

For a time in Europe she continued her painting, "working with batik on silk, dipping the colors in hot wax. I sold five or six works, realistic, not abstract—mountain scenes, villages, castles, things I remember from the Cascades in Washington or from traveling around Europe. No painting lately, though. I've been busy making curtains for eighteen windows in our house in Belgium."

When she was interviewed in 1983 Anne Anderson said that they had no immediate plans for children, "but we've got to get going soon —I'm twenty-eight years old." Children, she feared, would keep her at home while Anderson was out racing. "I don't want to miss this," she said. "Philip is working so hard, and I want to help him." In 1984 she was pregnant, proud of it, and back with the Tour.

○

For Bastille Day, fireworks lit the night sky over Grenoble, once described by Stendhal, a native son, as a mudhole, but now a city of 160,000. The riders were dispersed at hotels outside town, and none seemed to have made their way to the banks of the Isère River to watch a high-tech laser-beam depiction of the fall of the Bastille fortress to revolutionaries in 1789. Smoke bombs exploded, dogs howled, small children wept with fright and fatigue as the night grew late, and the blue and red light shafts played over the Alpine foothills. Tomorrow the Tour would pass that way for the start of its final week. "Barteau has been in the yellow jersey because the favorites have been waiting for the Alps," said Gerard Veldscholten, a Dutchman with the Panasonic team. "Now the real race begins."

Vincent Barteau still held a significant lead, but not one that could withstand a bad day in the mountains: 10 minutes 13 seconds over Laurent Fignon. Barteau had held up far better than his two companions on the Cergy-Pontoise breakaway. Maurice Le Guilloux ranked thirty-third overall, and the Portuguese Paulo Ferreira, last by nearly an hour in the one day in the Pyrenees, had been so exhausted by the effort that he fell further behind each succeeding day until here in Grenoble he ranked last in the field of 140 men who remained in the race—*la lanterne rouge,* the figurative red lantern that marked the end of the train. Third behind Barteau and Fignon was Hinault, 12 minutes 26 seconds behind Barteau, with Veldscholten fourth, 12 minutes 28 seconds behind, and Phil Anderson fifth, 13 minutes 17 seconds behind. Greg LeMond was sixth, 14 minutes 23 seconds behind; Sean Kelly seventh, 14 minutes 27 seconds behind; Pedro Delgado eighth, 14 minutes 37 seconds behind; Robert Millar ninth, 14 minutes 56 seconds behind; and Peter Winnen tenth, 16 minutes 42 seconds behind. Some of the better climbers were near the top ten, with Angel Arroyo eleventh, Pascal Simon fifteenth, Eric Caritoux sixteenth, and Luis Herrera twenty-second, 21 minutes 49 seconds behind.

Herrera had been a disappointment so far and his Colombian team a bust, criticized by other riders and team officials. "The Colombians refuse to work," complained Peter Post, the manager of the Panasonic team. "They just sit there and let everybody else do the work. From them, nothing."

The trouble may have been not in themselves but in their stars. Dr. Ebel Botero Escobar, the biorhythm specialist and columnist for *La Patria,* the leading newspaper in Manizales, Colombia, had warned that the team faced a difficult time in the Tour. Dr. Botero Escobar made his reputation in his motherland by predicting, to the day, when Herrera would be forced to quit Colombia's Clásica Cundinamaraca in the spring, so in Manizales and as far afield as Medellín and even Bogotá, people listened when he spoke. "Only a miracle will allow Herrera to win the Tour," he predicted before the race, consulting the rider's triple curves of physical, psychological, and emotional form. "It's even improbable that Herrera will reach Paris."

The omens were equally grave for Fignon. "It is very doubtful that Fignon can duplicate his efforts in last year's Tour," Dr. Botero Escobar decided. The charts pointed to an inverse trajectory for the Frenchman, especially from July 13 through July 15, the day after Bastille Day. Fignon's only hope seemed to be that the Colombian had read his charts upside down. On the eve of the dread days, coming into the Domaine du Rouret in the fourteenth stage, Hinault was leading the gang finish nearly 18 minutes behind De Wolf when Fignon shot by him to finish an easy second. "That's when Fignon most astonished me," said Raymond Poulidor, fourteen times a competitor in the Tour. "Hinault attacked at the end of the race and Fignon

Bernard Hinault glances back and sees that he has not dropped Laurent Fignon on the road to L'Alpe-d'Huez (seventeenth stage).

Luis Herrera of the Colombian team leading a climb in the Alps.

Vincent Barteau of the Renault team.

A fan runs alongside Bernard Hinault at L'Alpe-d'Huez, shouting encouragement.

Laurent Fignon passes through the hundreds of thousands who line the route to L'Alpe-d'Huez (seven-teenth stage).

Through the Alps, past fields of perpetual snow.

Through the Alps.

Jock Boyer of the Skil team being encouraged by fellow Americans in the Alps.

Skylarking in the ranks—Pascal Poisson of the Renault team wears a traffic cone on his head on the way out of Switzerland (twenty-first stage).

Vincent Barteau of Renault playfully holds back his teammate, Laurent Fignon, as the pack enjoys a break (twenty-first stage).

COR VOS

The pack on the Champs-Elysées (twenty-third and last stage).

Eric Vanderaerden of Panasonic-Raleigh wins the final sprint, in Paris.

Laurent Fignon of Renault and Marianne Martin of the American team hoist their trophies in Paris.

countered him, taking over the sprint and winning it with a laughable ease from an Hinault who was really rolling, believe me."

Fignon was missing no opportunity to attempt to impress, perhaps even intimidate, Hinault. The next day, again with victory out of reach, Fignon dominated the pack finish in the fifteenth stage, into Grenoble, winding up third behind Frédéric Vichot of Skil and Michel Laurent of Coop. His biorhythms might be down but he was most people's favorite in both the individual time trial on July 15 and the rest of the race.

"Fignon should win," Veldscholten felt, "with Hinault second." Down the table in the Panasonic team's hotel, Phil Anderson agreed: "Hinault is strong but he doesn't have the kick, the zap, that Fignon does." LeMond no longer spoke as if he had a real chance left. "In the Alps, anything can happen," he said, trying to sound hopeful before he let a glimmer of his disappointment show. "Right now I'd be happy to be in the first five in Paris." Despite the handful of minutes separating the first ten riders, it had come down to a two-man race.

The coming five days would settle all questions. First on the program was a 22-kilometer individual time trial, then the climbs to L'Alpe-d'Huez, La Plagne, and Morzine, followed by an incursion into Switzerland and its Alps at Crans-Montana. Hinault was publicly optimistic, predicting that after Fignon's rigorous Tour of Italy, he could be expected to have at least one bad day in the mountains. "I've only two minutes on Hinault, and that's not much, considering the mountains," Fignon admitted. "The least weakness will cost me a lot."

Both riders appeared to be relaxed the day before the sixteenth stage, a time trial at La Ruchère-en-Chartreuse, just outside Grenoble —the first half entirely flat and the second half climbing nearly 800 meters in a distance so short that the ascent was judged to be beyond classification on the scale of difficulty. A sign of the riders' tension, however, was furnished when the organizers decided to waive the rule that, to discourage relays, forbade a rider to precede or follow a teammate in a time trial. According to this rule, Fignon, ranking second, could not precede Barteau, but would have to switch starts with Hinault. Citing another rule, one that allowed them to waive any rule, the organizers decided late the night before the race to allow Hinault, Fignon, and Barteau to leave in that order, 3 minutes apart.

Nothing would have changed the race. Herrera had had the fastest run, with Delgado second and Hinault third, when Fignon came storming up the mountain through the lane left among 100,000 spectators. Hinault had had the fastest times at kilometer 12, the last on the flat, and at kilometer 16, but Fignon was 1 second better at the first point and 3 seconds better at the second. Then he flew, finishing 25 seconds faster than Herrera, 32 seconds faster than Delgado, and 35 seconds faster than Hinault. The margin was nowhere so impressive as the manner: sprinting the last few hundred meters, he crossed the finish line and immediately glanced down at the watch on his left wrist. Everybody else had arrived gasping and sucking for breath, but Fignon was cool enough to check his time. When reporters reached him, he was articulate. Yes, he said, there had been a bad moment early in the climb: "I became a little unglued, and for five hundred or six hundred meters I couldn't keep my rhythm." He had not panicked. "When things come unstuck, you try to stay cool. You come up empty —it doesn't last long if you're well trained. You have to remember that." Were there any other questions?

Hinault was angry, complaining that he had been forced to leave before Fignon despite the rule. "Fignon based his race on mine," he said. "That's what you do to keep something in reserve and finish strong. If we had gone off with him ahead, I would have based my race on his, and I would have won. The whole affair upset me. I slept badly, I was nervous. I wanted to win for the public."

His listeners were astonished. Hinault, who always before had said, "I race only for myself," was now talking about offering a victory to his fans. "The public is being nicer to me these days," he confessed. "In France you have to lose to be loved."

When *a great tree falls, it creates a* mighty noise.

From the start of the seventeenth stage, a 151-kilometer climb to L'Alpe-d'Huez, Bernard Hinault had based his strategy on isolating Laurent Fignon from his teammates, forcing Fignon to stay with him until he was exhausted, then discarding his young challenger many minutes behind. In principle, the strategy was sound. Fignon had had a grueling Tour of Italy, had been kept on edge for nearly two weeks by Hinault's many forays in the Tour de France and had been known to experience an off day in the mountains—*un jour sans,* as the riders called it, a day without. He had a history of *jours sans*, most recently during the Tour of Italy.

Riding as always near the front, Hinault attacked early, during the first major climb toward the Col du Coq peak. It was not enough to send a Vie Claire teammate ahead, for Fignon would respond by sending one of his Renault crew; Hinault had to offer himself as the bait, dangling the possibility that he would break away and leave Fignon behind. It was their private duel. Radio Tour, which links all cars and offers periodic reports on the race, spoke of nobody but Hinault and Fignon for most of the day.

Fignon had his team working strongly, and each time Hinault feinted, he was quickly rejoined. About 45 kilometers from the finish, on the Côte de Laffrey, Hinault resumed the attack, pulling away five times during the ascent of a hill half the size of L'Alpe-d'Huez but no less steep. "I'm a fighter, a real fighter," Hinault was to say when the day was done. "I never accept defeat, and as long as I breathe, I attack." Five times Fignon overtook him, but the strategy had its desired effect of stretching out the pack into small groups, some far to the rear, leaving Fignon at last isolated from his teammates. The six riders at the front were Hinault, Fignon, and four of the strongest climbers in the race: Luis Herrera of Colombia; Angel Arroyo, a Spanish rider with the Reynolds team; Robert Millar of Peugeot; and Beat Breu of Cilo-Aufina, the Swiss team.

Then it was Fignon's turn to attack. Breaking away with Herrera, he built a 48-second lead on the descent, only to have Hinault and his group overhaul them with about 20 kilometers to go, about 7 short of the L'Alpe-d'Huez climb. "The art of being now very audacious, now very prudent is the art of succeeding," said Napoleon, who had passed this way himself in 1815 during his hundred glorious days from Elba to Waterloo. Facing this choice, Hinault went for audacity and attacked, sprinting away from Fignon and Herrera. "When I saw that," Fignon related later, "I had a good laugh. It's the truth. I really broke up. It was crazy. When you've been outdistanced, the least you can do when you overtake is catch your breath. But Bernard has too much pride. He really wanted to dazzle everybody. Anybody could have told him he had no chance to pull anything off, that his game was lost from the start."

So it was. Hinault built a mere 26-second lead, which was worn away speedily as the riders started climbing to L'Alpe-d'Huez. If he was seeking the proper theater, Hinault had chosen well: the premier Alpine finish, the one that traditionally weeds out the contenders, for thirty years the place where the Tour was not always won but where it was usually lost. Legend said that in the early 1950s, two scouts for the Tour drove up the dirt roads to L'Alpe-d'Huez in the winter, got out of their car at the small ski resort near the 1,860-meter-high summit, and simply stared at each other in awe. L'Alpe-d'Huez has been on the race calendar ever since. Its roads have been graded and paved, but its twenty-two hairpin turns are no less fearsome now than then, especially with half a million people lining the ramps, pouring water over the riders, running alongside them to shout encouragement, clapping them on the back, giving those in trouble on the climb an illegal push. Some of this is welcomed by most riders, like the bottle of mineral water poured over their heads. Some of it is simply dangerous—like the slap of encouragement, which can break a rider's concentration and rhythm—or demoralizing—like seeing a spectator running faster than the rider can go on his bicycle. All of it is part of the L'Alpe-d'Huez climb.

As the road mounted through the crowds, Hinault was passed by Herrera, his small body hunched over his swaying bicycle, his baby-bird's face intent on the road ahead. Then it was Fignon's turn to pass out of sight. Later came Millar, then Rafael Acevedo of Colombia, and finally, in the last kilometer, Greg LeMond. Hinault finished sixth, nearly 4 minutes behind Herrera, the winner, and 3 minutes behind the second-place Fignon.

Hinault has never been a pure climber—whatever that means, since nobody can quite define the type. Most outstanding climbers are smallish men with an outsize chest and breathing capacity, but some-times they are larger and their strength comes from their legs instead of their lungs. Sometimes they are from the mountains of Spain and Switzerland and sometimes from tabletop country, like Belgium or the Netherlands or Hinault's native Brittany. Sometimes they are grace and finesse personified and sometimes have only raw power. Hinault had a bit of all these virtues and could be relied on not so much to win, which he rarely did in the mountains, as not to lose much time. Climb-ing is a matter of concentration, riders say, a test of character, of ability to suffer. Like all champions, Hinault knew how to suffer and gloried in this ability. What he needed around him were riders to set a pace he could adjust to, engines to which he could join as part of a train. Disastrously, he had attempted to become the engine.

"Bernard really made a stupid mistake," his former manager, Cy-rille Guimard, said. "He went all out to gain twenty-six seconds, which translated into a three-minute loss. I think that if he had stayed with the others and not attacked, he would have been left behind on the climb but would have lost only a minute." Even LeMond, Hinault's friend and former protege, was stunned when he heard of the attack in the valley, judging it a sign that Hinault had no confidence in his strength up the mountain. One of Hinault's few defenders was Millar, who seemed to share his sense of drama. "It wasn't stupid to attack as soon as we rejoined Fignon," Millar insisted. "That was absolutely the moment to take your chances. The way it worked out, Hinault just didn't have the strength left. He bet the whole bundle on one chance. He failed, but it was the only way to beat Fignon."

Atop the mountain, Herrera had become the first amateur and the first Colombian to win a stage in the Tour de France. Breaking out a thicket of flags, the Colombian press corps and other supporters dashed in all directions to spread the word, broadcasting it back home halfway around the world. On the victory podium, Fignon put on the yellow jersey in the same town where he first donned it the year before. "It's the first one that you remember all your life," he said. "It's less thrilling today than it was a year ago. Maybe it's because I knew I would get the yellow jersey in the Alps. Whether it was here or farther along didn't make much difference, but I was certain I would get it."

The beaten Hinault acknowledged that he knew it too, as soon as Fignon overtook him during the climb. "By then I had no illusions left," he said. "I knew I wouldn't be able to stay with him. I attacked a dozen times during the day; I gave it all I had and there wasn't much left. Fignon is a racer, all right. Both of us took all risks possible, and I lost. But that's the game. I bet everything, but that's cycling."

○

"His glorious adventure," they all called the two weeks Vincent Barteau had spent in the yellow jersey, and at the end of the 2,200 kilometers from Cergy-Pontoise to L'Alpe-d'Huez, Barteau finally agreed with them. He had been slow in coming around. When he lost the three-man breakaway to Paulo Ferreira on the fifth day of the Tour, he had been beyond consolation. "Of course I'm disappointed," he said as he slipped on the overall leader's yellow jersey for the first time. "I wanted the stage victory. The only thing that counts is going across the line with your arms up.

Most riders gave Barteau about a week to enjoy his leadership. "He ought to keep the jersey until the mountains, but no longer," said Greg LeMond, who rode with the faltering Barteau in the mountains of the Dauphiné Libéré earlier in the spring. "Oh, there," Barteau could say later, dismissively. "In the Dauphiné I had no motivation. In the Tour it was all open before me."

He was discovering on the road to the mountains what so many other riders have learned, that the yellow jersey is a wonderful inspiration. Alone in yellow, the leader is easy to spot as the pack whizzes by and the spectators yell an "*Allez*." And before each morning's start, when the riders gather in the town's main square and have a few minutes to spend chatting with the locals, who can a fan more want to be photographed with than the yellow jersey? Barteau was gracious, making time for these moments, but still a faceless leader, the surrogate for LeMond, Bernard Hinault, Laurent Fignon, or whoever was going to emerge from the Pyrenees as the real leader.

"The biggest thrill was to come home to Normandy in the yellow jersey," Barteau recalled. "And then to do well in the Pyrenees, where I surprised myself." On the road to Guzet-Neige, he surprised everybody by finishing nineteenth, only 4 minutes 10 seconds behind the winner, Robert Millar, barely half a minute behind LeMond, 1 minute behind Hinault, and not quite two minutes behind Fignon.

With a 10-minute lead still left over Fignon, Barteau had seemed to be a real factor in the race, as Merckx and Fignon judged it. "He has begun to understand his possibilities," his Renault teammate said. "Can I imagine him winning the Tour? Why not?"

Who is this Barteau? the fans asked, knowing only that he was a second-year professional in his first Tour. "I'm happy and spontaneous," Barteau explained in countless interviews once he had begun to be taken seriously. "If I hadn't become a bicycle racer, I would have joined the circus. I'm just kidding. I kid about a lot of things, but when it comes to bicycling, I'm serious." As a boy he had played soccer and run cross-country at first, but turned to bicycling because he came from a family of cyclists. His father, Henri, who had also been his coach, had been an amateur rider of distinction in Normandy, as had been Barteau's two older brothers and an uncle. As became Vincent Barteau himself: between 1974 and 1982 he won 200 races, was three times champion of Normandy in different age groups, and the French junior champion in 1980. "But when you become a pro," he said, "none of that counts. You start at zero."

Barteau well remembered his first victory in the Normandy championship. "I was in high school, learning to become a furnace repairman in Caen, seven A.M. to seven P.M., and I was bored. One day in 1976 I was looking out the window and watching the sun and grass, and I just wanted to get outside. So in the middle of class I packed my briefcase and left. The teacher said, 'Where are you going, Barteau? You'll be sorry.'

"I couldn't help myself. I went home by bus, got on my bike, rode a hundred kilometers, and said to myself, How am I going to explain this to my father? But he was great. He just said, 'Let's start getting ready for the championships.' And two weeks later I was the champion."

With his snub nose, open face, and blond hair falling over his forehead, Barteau resembles the fresh kid, the wise guy, who sat in the back of everybody's high school class, never knowing the answers, usually sassing the teacher. In conversation, he is deeper than that, sincere and realistic. Immediately after the Pyrenees, he was able to say about the Alps, "That will certainly be the end of my adventure. Let me be in the yellow jersey until then and I'll give it up willingly. I've been living day to day, and each evening, when the stage is over, is a time of great happiness. There will be time to think later."

The time had come in L'Alpe-d'Huez, where Barteau finished a creditable fifty-third, 11 minutes 40 seconds behind Herrera, and dropped to second place overall, 4 minutes 22 seconds behind Fignon and 1 minute 19 seconds ahead of the third-place Hinault. Barteau's father was ready, having traveled with him since the weekend before. "He's going to need me soon," the father had said. "When he loses the yellow jersey, he'll need some comforting. He's still only a kid, you know."

The kid stood by with a sweet smile as Fignon slipped into the yellow jersey and he took the white one, signifying that he was still the leading first-time rider in the Tour. Barteau did not expect even that jersey to be his property for long. "I'm just keeping it for LeMond," he joked. He did not need to mention that when the Tour paused, nobody looked for the white jersey or beseeched him to please move a bit closer for a photograph. The yellow jersey made the difference. "I've realized a kid's dream." he said. "I keep seeing myself closing the curtains at home so I could watch the Tour better on television when I was a kid.

"At Cergy-Pontoise I didn't understand what the yellow jersey meant," Barteau admitted. "Now I wouldn't trade it for a hundred thousand stage victories. I've worn it almost two weeks and I realize that at age twenty-two in my first Tour, it's been a wonderful experience. I've proven that I'm not a clown and that I don't owe everything to luck. I think I've proven my courage."

"I relaxed a lot after losing the jersey," Barteau said some weeks later. "The pressure was so great, the television people every day, the newspapermen, the fans. Once I lost the jersey I had a different goal, helping Fignon and LeMond, and making sure I finished. It was inspiring just to finish, it was superb." There had been many invitations for post-Tour critériums in villages; "Everybody wants to see Barteau," he said.

"I'm young and I'm good," he continued. "My goal now is to win a classic—Paris-Roubaix maybe. I have to be relaxed, liberated, to be at my best, and I think the yellow jersey gave me that liberty. What the experience really taught me was to have confidence in myself. My father always used to say, 'You don't believe enough in yourself.' Now I do."

○

Everybody loves a winner and being a winner, except Hubert Linard of the Peugeot team. Linard was outraged when he learned in the middle of the Tour that he had been awarded the victory in the spring's Bordeaux-Paris race because Marcel Tinazzi, who finished first, had been disqualified after a positive drug test. A rider unaccustomed to triumph, Linard was bitter that it had taken so long to change the final standings. In the forty-five days since Bordeaux-Paris, Tinazzi had presumably signed many contracts for August critériums, while Linard obviously had not. Now the market was nearly closed, awaiting only those riders who attracted attention in the Tour de France. Linard was struggling badly in the Tour, and his outrage was understandable. "I was disappointed to finish second in Bordeaux-Paris, and now I'm even more disappointed to be named the winner," he said. "I've been cheated out of my victory."

Taking a rare moral position among professional riders, he was also angry that Tinazzi had used stimulants. "Tinazzi didn't have the right to cheat in a race that big," Linard charged. "Bordeaux-Paris doesn't deserve this."

Tinazzi, who was not riding in the Tour, issued a denial that he had taken any of the long list of substances banned by the International Cycling Union and its French federation. Thus they always say, and sometimes truthfully. Or so it must be believed. There are so many opportunities to cheat—to fake exhaustion, to swerve at the wrong instant and let an opponent through, to finish unaccountable minutes behind in a climb—that if the riders were not regarded as truthful, what hope could there be that professional bicycling was any more honest than professional wrestling? And to what would the fan be giving his heart?

A standard denial could be the one made by Raymond Martin after he was disqualified in the 1982 Tour de l'Avenir: "I didn't cheat, I swear it. It's true that I treated myself"—the verb racers always use. "Like everybody, I've been following the same treatment for eleven years. Believe me, if I had anything to hide, I wouldn't have sprinted like a madman to finish second, and I wouldn't have been checked." In most races, the first three or four finishers are checked by urinalysis for illegal substances, but in the Tour the daily tests extend to the yellow jersey at the start of the stage, the first two finishers of the stage, and two riders drawn by lot. Martin's argument was common: Why would a rider, knowing he had taken a stimulant or painkiller, try to win a race if thereby he faced a drug check? One answer is that if he didn't hope to win, why would he take the stimulant? Or did he get carried away in the final charge to the line? Even the riders appear not to know the answers to these questions.

During the professional season, from February to October, riders are exposed to wind, rain, and even snow as they log up to 250 kilometers a day, often in the mountains. They feel tired and they get sick, and often they are treated with some of the many drugs banned by the sport's officials. Riders are occasionally caught by urinalysis and then penalized: Angel Arroyo was stripped of his victory in the 1982 Tour of Spain, the Vuelta, and Eric McKenzie of his victory in the Grand Prix of Zurich.

Another standard denial came from Walter Godefroot, then manager of the Capri-Sonne team, after McKenzie was disqualified: "He swore to me he took nothing and he's no liar. But he showed traces of cortisone and he was probably the unwitting victim of a careless *soigneur*" (the masseur, sometimes a former rider, who can advise riders about medical problems, since so few teams include a doctor). A couple of decades ago, before there were drug tests or the 1966 French law that makes it illegal to consume, prescribe, or offer a multitude of drugs that improve an athlete's performance, the riders believed generally in treating or taking care of themselves. "Cortisone is nothing," Roger

Pingeon, the winner of the 1967 Tour, said a few years ago. "If you give your body the dose of cortisone it needs, no problem. That's what's called balancing, not doping."

A few years ago one of these old-timers was talking about his team's plans for the day off in L'Alpe-d'Huez during the Tour. "We'll sleep a bit later than usual, then the team will go down the mountain, ride forty or fifty kilometers on the flat, and finish up by climbing this bloody hill again," he said. "Then we'll eat a late lunch, have a massage, and spend the rest of the day relaxing."

Wouldn't he rather spend the entire day in bed? he was asked.

"Of course I would," he answered, "but you don't dare do it. You've got to go out every day on the bike and work up a sweat to burn the poisons out. I hate climbing this hill"—he gestured at the window—"but if you didn't have it, you'd have to do ninety or a hundred kilometers on the flat. The thing is not to let a day go by without giving the system a chance to throw off the poisons. You've got to sweat them out." Poisons or medication—nobody ever calls it doping.

Only hours after this conversation, the leader of the 1978 Tour, Michel Pollentier of the Flandria team, was disqualified in L'Alpe-d'Huez when he was caught attempting to defraud the drug test after he took a banned substance. The news was sensational not because he had used the drug but because never before had a leader of the Tour been eliminated for fraud. After winning the stage up the mountain, Pollentier did not go immediately to the urinalysis trailer but to his hotel, where he donned a long-sleeved jersey to conceal a small flask containing another person's urine sample. This flask was hidden in Pollentier's right armpit, while a rubber tube led down his arm to his wrist.

What happened when he arrived nearly an hour late for the test is still told different ways years later. There are various versions of who was in the room, but most stories include Pollentier, a Dr. Calvez of the French bicycling federation, and an inspector, Renato Sacconi, of the International Cycling Union. Despite the rules, which ordered a rider to be bare from the neck to the shoulders to discourage fraud, Pollentier is usually described as having been allowed to wear his jersey. Most versions agree that he could not get the apparatus to work and that, as he fumbled and flapped his arm to squeeze the flask, he was suddenly seized by the doctor, who pulled up his sleeve and revealed the tubing. Some versions, including Pollentier's own, say that the doctor removed the apparatus and allowed the rider to fill the flask with his own urine.

Near tears during an impromptu press conference the next day, Pollentier told a confused story, seeming uncertain exactly what his offense had been. As questions were put to him in several languages, he appeared to be contrite, self-pitying, and resentful, charging that of course French doctors were hostile to Belgian riders. This was not the first time he had been involved in a drug controversy; he had been disqualified from the Tour of Lombardy in Italy in 1974 and from the Tour of Belgium in 1977 for having used illegal stimulants. Speaking of the new charge, he said, "The medication I took is to help me breathe. I've used it before; it isn't an amphetamine." In fact it was called Alupent, and pharmacists in Paris identified it as an aid to asthmatics, said it was available by prescription only, and warned strongly against using it without a doctor's supervision. Alupent was especially dangerous for heart patients. Pollentier said he had taken the drug to help him during the long, hot climb through the Alps and admitted that he had also used it in the Tours of Switzerland and Italy, both of which he won the year before. He added that Alupent had not shown up on the detection scale used in those two races. "There is nothing wrong with my specimen," he insisted. "They took my specimen and there was no trouble with it. The doctor said it was acceptable. I signed and countersigned for it."

Nearly overlooked in the uproar, a bicyclist chosen at random, the seventy-seventh-placed Antoine Gutierrez, was also discovered with something up his sleeve. It all recalled the hoary Tour joke: The rider is told that he has passed the doping test and, incidentally, congratulations, he's pregnant.

Among the riders there was a tendency to blame the inspections for encouraging, even forcing, them to cheat. Even those who use no drugs are bitter that the list of banned substances is so long and that they are the only professional athletes tested daily for stimulants. "I went to the pharmacist's to buy a cough syrup for my little boys," Bernard Hinault has often said. "Luckily, before I used it myself, I looked at the label and saw it contained substances banned for a professional bicycle racer." Another spokesman for this point of view is Jacques Anquetil, who thundered in his column after the Pollentier affair: "I do not wish to hear spoken the word 'doping.' One must say rather 'treating yourself,' and speak of treatments that are not appropriate for ordinary mortals. You cannot compete in the Tour de France on mineral water alone." What Anquetil did not mention in his frequent attacks on drug testing, but what most readers remembered, was that he lost a world record in a one-hour race against the clock in 1967 by refusing to appear for a doping test until 48 hours after the event.

The Pollentier affair occurred nearly a decade ago, and no case of fraud has been reported since by the Tour, although, as in Joop Zoetemelk's case, positive drug tests are not uncommon. Sometimes the rumors still go around that the riders' urine samples are proving positive but that the French federation doctors have been instructed to be lenient, or that some teams' doctors are so far ahead of the federation doctors that the stimulants used today do not show up in the chemical analysis. From time to time, a race will even be run without drug tests, an illegal practice but one never punished. Occasionally, too, a rider will hint that he left a team because of its medical practices, without saying more.

Speaking about the Pollentier affair, Paul Sherwen, an English rider, then with the Fiat team and now with La Redoute, admitted that the change from amateur racing to professional had been complicated by problems of medication. "I never took the vitamins before that I take now," he said in his first year with the Tour de France. "People were always saying that vitamin B_1 was essential, but I never bothered with it. Winning was simple enough without it. Now I take my shots like everybody else. I couldn't last in a race like this without them. But no doping. At the start of the season, the Fiat team manager checked all our suitcases for pills. That's out with Fiat—very definitely out."

Coincidentally or not, the Fiat team was ninth in the eleven-team field in overall points in 1978, and last in time accrued in the race. Shortly thereafter it disbanded. As everybody said, Fiat might as well have been riding for the exercise.

THIRTEEN

Not everybody was pleased with the way

Laurent Fignon had mocked Bernard Hinault after the climb to L'Alpe-d'Huez, but Fignon seemed to believe that if you couldn't kick a man when he was down, when could you kick him? Even while he talked offhandedly and modestly about himself, he was unable to skip an opportunity to needle his rival. "I don't know if I'm becoming one of the great riders," he told an interviewer, "but I do know that it all ends one day. Look at Bernard. Two years ago they called him unbeatable."

By the end of the eighteenth stage, a 185-kilometer climb through the Alps from L'Alpe-d'Huez to the ski resort of La Plagne, this amounted nearly to bear baiting, with Hinault the chained bear. He'd had a bad day—even he admitted so—and yet he was still able to growl: "They say I'm riding stupidly. But I don't care if I finish an hour behind, because I'm not one of those riders who shoot for second place. Let everybody know it: I don't give a damn for second place." By now he was hurt physically and psychologically. At age twenty-nine he needed more than one night's sleep to recover from the strains of the L'Alpe-d'Huez climb. Fignon could proclaim that he was pleased the day off had come before the climb, rather than after, because he thought a break now would only reduce his power; Hinault was among those aching.

He was also wounded. Nobody was willing to confirm it, but the rumor said that as the pack began to climb the 2,640-meter-high Col du Galibier, the struggling Hinault had been jeered by riders who recalled with bitterness his breakaways on the road to Bordeaux, to Blagnac, and to L'Alpe-d'Huez. Another version of the rumor went that they had not so much mocked him as tried to shame him into not attacking and allowing the pack to have a paced, uneventful day. Any professional can stay with the pack when it is rolling at a steady 40 kilometers an hour; the losses begin when the speed jumps back and forth from 30 kilometers to 60. With three imposing climbs ahead, all rated beyond classification for height and difficulty, and two long and steep descents, nobody wanted another day of attacks and counterattacks. The consensus was that the race had ended and all that remained was to follow Fignon through the Alps and back to Paris. Discussing the pack's mentality, the rider Bernard Vallet once said: "Uppermost there's a solidarity that you have to respect or the pack will be on you. If we're going up a mountain and everybody knows you've got to take it slowly, it will be regarded very badly if somebody attacks. There are conventions, not laws, but you've got to respect them: a rider doesn't attack during a stop to urinate or after a spill."

Nobody need have worried on the way up. Hinault was in trouble, reaching the top in fortieth place, 3 minutes 50 seconds behind the leaders, including Fignon, who was having another splendid day. He climbed like a sightseer, he said later, taking time to admire the grand view across the top of the Alpine world. In a car following the riders, all the clichés were uttered: The Pyrenees are lovely mountains, human in their scale, but the Alps are truly majestic, dominating, forcing man to feel insignificant.

At this height the snow was aged and frozen nearly as hard as stone. Across the valleys, it looked white, but close up it had turned gray. Hundreds of bicycles leaned against the snowbanks of the Galibier, placed there by the amateur riders who wanted to match their times against the professionals', and were happy to overlook the toll of riding the first two weeks of the Tour. Here and there in the snowbanks, as they did every year, spectators had written the names of their favorites, picking out the letters in stone and mud. Fignon pronounced the view "super," and well worth the climb. "From time to time," he added, "I looked back down to see where Hinault was."

Once over the top, Fignon had no need to look back. Hinault stormed into the descent, unable to resist attacking at 80 kilometers an hour on a road awash in loose gravel and the runoff from the glaciers above. He made up the lost minutes on the leaders and then, with 25 kilometers of open road before the next climb, went off alone on another doomed breakaway into a strong wind. The Vie Claire trainer, Paul Koechli, drove up to Hinault and attempted to reason with him, but finally he had to shrug and drop back. Hinault had gained a minute's lead before the Renault team caught up to him. "Why should I be disappointed?" Koechli asked. "We'll continue to take risks. If we weren't here, what kind of race would it have been? Fignon in the yellow jersey by half an hour." Hinault sounded bitter about this chase, complaining that he was obviously not having a good day and that therefore Renault should have allowed him the liberty of flight. What was his old team so worried about?

The answer became known after the next climb, up to the 1,990-meter-high Col de la Madeleine and its abandoned landscape of shepherds' huts and ruined barns, their roofs long collapsed and their stone walls tumbling back down the slopes where they were quarried. Again Hinault was dropped on the climb, and again he recovered on the descent. But the next climb, up to the final destination of La Plagne, finished on the top.

The winner, by an easy 1 minute 4 seconds, was Fignon. "I wanted to win a stage in the Alps," he said. "I hoped it would be yesterday at L'Alpe-d'Huez, but that wasn't possible. So today I went for it again." He might have won even more handily, but he seemed to have hesitated on the climb as Jean-Marie Grézet, a Swiss rider with the Skil team, broke away. Fignon was waiting for Greg LeMond to take off after Grézet. Renault strategy—Fignon's and Guimard's—called for LeMond to be given every opportunity to make up time on Hinault and finish ahead of him when the race reached Paris. With 12 kilometers to go, in full sight of the hideous skyscrapers that were planted at the summit and proclaimed a resort, Fignon realized that LeMond could not overtake Grézet, now 2 minutes 14 seconds ahead. So the yellow jersey sped off, catching and dropping Grézet in 6 kilometers. How easy it seemed if the spectators watched only Fignon and not the riders who straggled in long afterward, some of them making it because of illegal pushes or because they had the sense to drop back and shelter behind the team cars following the winners.

Luis Herrera, yesterday's hero, was complaining of kidney trouble and had needed an injection just to start. He finished 20 minutes late. Paulo Ferreira, the Portuguese winner at Cergy-Pontoise and *la lan-*

terne rouge since Grenoble, was so far behind that he was disqualified on time differential with the winners. Phil Anderson wobbled in twenty-fifth. Since his fall on the descent into Grenoble, he had been in pain and found climbing almost unbearable. Fourth overall after the time trial at La Ruchère-en-Chartreuse, he had fallen to eighth place at L'Alpe-d'Huez and now to thirteenth.

His wife had done her best to help him. "I saw Philip and he was in a lot of pain, but the uncertainty was even worse," Anne Anderson said before the La Plagne climb. "The *soigneur* said that if anything was broken, there was nothing they could do. But they hadn't even done an X ray. Philip spent two days in pain, having to stop by the side of the road, panicked because he couldn't breathe on the climbs. So I went down to the hotel's front desk and asked if there was a doctor in L'Alpe-d'Huez with an X-ray machine. We found one and called him, and he said to come over—he found a bad bone bruise in the sternum, nothing broken but the bone pushed in and starting to come back. Two days to find out nothing was broken! He said a shot of cortisone in the bone would stop the pain; otherwise it would hurt for three weeks. Philip couldn't have the shot, of course, so he'll hurt for three weeks." Anderson was glassy-eyed when he crossed the finish line, more than 14 minutes behind Fignon, and a Panasonic *soigneur* gave him a towel. As the photographers grouped around him, the *soigneur* remembered to slip a team hat over Anderson's bare head. Without thinking about it, the stunned Anderson straightened the hat so that the team name showed.

Panasonic had its goals, Renault had its. In the last 7 kilometers, Guimard had pulled his car alongside LeMond and told him to attack. Grézet could be taken, and a substantial time gap opened over the tiring Hinault. LeMond tried hard but couldn't quite catch Grézet, finishing third, 3 seconds behind. Hinault trailed in nearly 2 minutes later, his lead over LeMond for second place down to 1 minute 13 seconds.

○

Even The Other American was talking about Greg LeMond. "My only regret, anyway the biggest one about LeMond," Jonathan Boyer said, "is that he doesn't do anything for U.S. cycling. He's said it himself— he rides for himself, he rides for money, he rides for a French team and then for America last. That's the wrong order."

Boyer was referring, at least partly, to the 1982 world championship at Goodwood, England. Wearing an American jersey, Boyer was ahead going into the final sprint when the man in the other American jersey, LeMond, led a charge that overtook Boyer. Teammates do not usually try to deprive each other of victory, but LeMond was unapologetic. "We were in the last five hundred meters and Boyer had only about a twenty-meter lead, which there was no way he could keep. I didn't think he could win it, and I didn't want him to. He's just not a friend. I didn't think he was the kind of guy who should be world champion. Boyer knew from the start of the race that we weren't friends and that we were both out for ourselves. I was wearing the U.S. jersey, sure, but there really wasn't a U.S. team and I definitely wasn't part of it. I paid for my own trip to England, my hotel bills, everything. There was no support from the U.S. federation. The team I was racing for was Renault."

However, Bernard Hinault, then Renault's leader, had dropped out long before, and as LeMond led the chase after Boyer, Giuseppe Saronni of Italy shot by and won the title by 5 seconds. LeMond took the silver medal as Boyer faded to finish tenth. LeMond won the world championship the next year in Switzerland.

LeMond's quarrel with Boyer dated to 1981, when he was being nurtured by Renault, and Boyer, who had come to Europe in his teens to learn with amateur bicycle teams, was hired not only as a rider but also as a fellow American and translator for LeMond, who supposedly spoke no French. He must have known a few words, since the story goes that he felt Boyer was mistranslating some answers to reporters' questions and putting him in a bad light. Boyer denied this. Whatever the cause, they had been estranged for years. "We haven't even talked for about four months," Boyer said in La Plagne. He seemed to be trying to avoid the controversies that had marked his career: his charge that LeMond still owed him money that Boyer earned helping LeMond win the world championship, the suspicion that he had caused the fall in which Pascal Simon had broken his shoulder blade in the 1983 Tour, the story that he had spilled a bottle of water on the ground rather than share it with a Colombian rider.

This year Boyer had other things on his mind. He was riding what he admitted was a humdrum Tour, around thirtieth place overall. "Some years you have it, some years you don't," Boyer said during the Skil team's dinner. "Which one this is for me is obvious. I've just been off. Physically I feel fine, the problem has been concentration. The falls ruined my concentration." He fell, he said, during the fourth stage, from Valenciennes to Béthune, and again during the La Ruchère time trial. He admitted that his outside activities also hampered his concentration.

The twenty-nine-year-old Boyer was deeply involved in Skil's plans to promote bicycle racing in the United States, Skil's headquarters in the power-tool business. The president of Skil said during the break in Grenoble that "Jock Boyer will be a key man in our promotion of cycling in America. That's basically why we brought him onto our team." After riding with the team for two seasons under the Sem jersey, Boyer switched in 1984 to a small Italian team, Brianzoli-Willer. "The year started well but finished badly when I cracked a vertebra in the Giro," he said. Shortly after that race in May, he was allowed to benefit from international bicycling rules and switch to Skil for the Tour de France; the rules allow a rider from a country with few teams, such as Switzerland or the United States, to ride for two teams during a season. Despite charges that he was simply a mercenary, mostly by Skil riders who were dropped for the Tour, Boyer came aboard. "The protests blew over quickly," he said in dismissal.

Now in his fourth Tour, Boyer had always been consistent in the mountains, usually in the top third or half of the pack. His best finish had been in 1983, twelfth place overall. "I do well in cycling, but I'm not Eddy Merckx. I never want to be somebody other than who I am," he said, spooning hills of crushed yeast over his soup and a platter of sliced tomatoes. When he started riding professionally in Europe, he was an exotic, the first American, sometimes called the Cowboy, perhaps because he was born in Utah and still spent winters in Wyoming, perhaps because the French feel any American not from their favorite cities of New York, San Francisco, or New Orleans has to be a cowboy. His eating habits attracted much attention, since he is nominally a vegetarian who mixes his own paste of fruit, nuts, and grains for intake during a race. He does eat some chicken and fish, he says, but no red meat.

Boyer also raises eyebrows in a traditionalist's sport by practicing yoga—"I do some yoga, but on the Tour it's difficult to get that going" —and by having a personal acupuncturist, whom he brought along on the race in 1983. "She couldn't come for this Tour because she's involved in a court case back home," he explained. "Somebody bit off her finger and she's suing." Instead he had to rely on the usual team masseurs, and complained in the Alps that his legs were painful.

"Anyway I'm just not on—the concentration and all that. It's my choice. I have nobody to blame but myself for getting in on the discussions about the Skil team in the United States. This is the right time to help U.S. cycling. It's got to get off to a good start." As cited by Skil officials, the statistics were impressive: $1 billion in annual U.S. sales of bicycles, 28 percent of all Americans owning or at least riding bicycles, the number of sales exceeding those of automobiles in almost every recent year. "I'll definitely race for Skil in the U.S.," Boyer said six months before plans for the team were dropped for money reasons. "Sure, all this planning has hurt my concentration. It's a distraction, but it's also my future."

Known as a man with his eye on the future, Boyer was noncommittal about whether he would continue to ride in future Tours de France. "The reason I ride is because I can't stop doing it," he said. "Then again, I might not ride next year but I'll be here for CBS." He has done racing commentary for television, "but I know I'm not good at it yet. I took some private speech courses in Carmel last year."

Boyer grew up and has long lived in the off-season in Carmel, California, where he operates a wholesale bicycle-equipment importing business in nearby Pebble Beach. He reported that business was booming. In Europe he lived for a few years near Annecy, in the Alps, but after his divorce, he sold his home there and accepted an invitation to live with the Skil team manager, Jean de Gribaldy. "I didn't really have a father—that is, my parents were divorced when I was five—so it fills a spot."

○

With the Tour de France assuredly won by Laurent Fignon, what did Greg LeMond think about the Renault team's new objective of pushing him into second place, ahead of Bernard Hinault, his former mentor and, in a boyish way, his idol? Despite this relationship, it would have been wrong to assume that LeMond was torn in his loyalties. He was a professional athlete and under professional discipline. The object was to win or come as close to winning as he could, and second place was closer than third.

In his public statements, LeMond hewed to the concept of team strategy. Discussing his lost chance to take the time that Laurent Fignon had tried to give him at La Plagne, LeMond defended his actions. "I might have gone after Fignon," he said, "or even attacked before him on the last climb. But that's not our game. I'm here now to get the best place I can, but also not to interfere with Laurent's plans. He's better than me in this race, and what's left for me is to try for a place on the podium—second, if possible.

"Laurent is on a higher level than me. He also has more experience in the Tour than I do. Maybe, with a bit of luck, I would be first on the team, but it doesn't bother me. A week ago, I was thinking of quitting, and now we're talking about second place for me. That's progress."

Talking about Hinault, LeMond was cautious and respectful. "Hinault is still a great champion," he said, "even if he's not where he was two years ago. I can imagine how hard it will be to overtake him because I can guess how hard he'll fight." LeMond rarely missed a chance to ride alongside Hinault in a quiet time of the race, perhaps near the start, and chat.

A strange rumor about the possibility of LeMond's switching teams was going around. It had started in Grenoble on the day off, traditionally the day when riders and teams make their commitments for the next season, far ahead of the legal opening of the transfer period to another team on October 1. Not surprisingly, this day of handshakes could complicate life for the remainder of the Tour and the fall classics. A rider for Team X, now secretly—and sometimes openly—committed to Team Y for next season, could find himself in an awkward position during a breakaway or climb with a rider for Team Y, nominally his rival but actually his future teammate—unless, of course, the Team Y rider was himself committed to Team Z. The riders had to keep their ears open to sort these movements out. The timing hurt the sport, everyone admitted, but few riders could afford to wait until October 1 to begin looking for a better-paying team. By then nearly all the jobs would be gone, and some teams too. It was common knowledge that Europ Décor would disband or cut far back next season, and the rumors said that Coop and Système U would also be gone. Some teams would remain but with new managers: Bernard Thévenet, twice a winner of the Tour de France, would probably be dismissed after his first season at La Redoute because of its dismal showing; Cilo-Aufina, the Swiss team, was also planning to change managers. At least one team was being formed for the next season, with Luis Ocana, the manager of the Teka team, planning to put together a group for Fagor, a Spanish manufacturer of electrical appliances.

With all these minuets, a rider had to be alert even if, like LeMond, he had another year to go on his Renault contract and was sharing the team leadership. "I think it's better for me to be on a team with two leaders," LeMond said. "If I'd been carrying all the responsibility this year, people would be disappointed in my performance. Fignon has been unbeatable. There's no reason Laurent and I can't continue to work well together." If not, the rumors said, it might even be Fignon himself who would be leaving.

This possibility had been raised by Bernard Tapie, the industrialist and sponsor of Hinault's Vie Claire team, while he was praising his star. "What if he does lose the Tour?" Tapie asked. "It's not that he's declined, but that Fignon has literally exploded this year. And what's so bad about having two Frenchmen at the top. Fignon is something, a real star." Seeing his opening, a reporter asked Tapie, "You'd like to have him work for you?" And Tapie had replied, "Obviously. I would give anything to have the chance once he's free." To which Cyrille Guimard, who never raided other teams, answered angrily the next day, "I was shocked to hear of Tapie's interest in Fignon. He likes to talk of a new world in bicycling, but nothing ever changes: holding a fat checkbook, he's ready to sign up a rider already under contract. All you can think is that Tapie, with all his talk about the future of bicycling, is just trying to get a little free publicity for his companies."

So the maneuvering for the next season continued; a rider really did need to keep informed. Better, a rider needed to do well. With his eagle's eye for financial opportunity, LeMond certainly hoped to capture second place.

That day's climb, 186 kilometers from La Plagne to yet another ski resort, Morzine, had changed nothing in the overall standings. Hinault had been active again, trying to energize a dull nineteenth stage over the sort of terrain that best suited him, five strong climbs, but none beyond classification, and five descents. Despite Fignon's efforts to let LeMond win the stage, they had finished in the same time as Hinault, 1 minute 14 seconds behind Angel Arroyo of the Reynolds team. Le-Mond had had a scare on the last descent, off the 1,713-meter-high Col de Joux-Plane, where tens of thousands of spectators lining the pass had left the narrowest of paths open on what was basically a back road in the country. For once the finish had not been at altitude but on the descent, and the riders were going all out, dodging spectators who wandered across the road and overflowed the curves. LeMond had gone off the road on a curve, spilling onto the grassy shoulder, unhurt. Less fortunate was Pedro Delgado, the Spaniard who liked to descend by leaning far over the handlebars to increase his speed. As he hung there, his front wheel punctured and he crashed. Cut and scraped, with his left shoulder aching, Delgado remounted and finished, a bit more than 4 minutes behind. When he was taken to a hospital, the doctors found that his shoulder was broken, and his race was over.

Far behind these leaders, Carlo Tonon was also rushing to get down the final peak. A twenty-nine-year-old Italian with the Carrera-Inoxpran team, Tonon ranked 111th overall among the 128 riders left in the race. If his object could not be victory, it could be, like LeMond's, to come as close to victory as possible; his team had promised him a bonus if he finished in the first one hundred when the race reached Paris. As he dashed downhill, did he wonder about a job for next year or marvel that he was even in the Tour de France, a last-minute re-placement after a Carrera sprinter was injured just before the team left Italy? Or did he ask why the team had even entered the race, the only one from Italy to do so? Or why it had remained in the Tour after its leader, Roberto Visentini, was forced to withdraw after being in-jured in a fall a week before? With no real reason to be there at all, Tonon turned into a curve and collided with a spectator who had wandered into the road on his bicycle, thinking that all the racers had passed. Both men were knocked unconscious and rushed by helicopter to a nearby hospital in grave condition. It was weeks before Tonon, recovering from a fractured skull, was fit enough to be taken home, and months before he could think of riding a bicycle again and planning with which team to spend his next season.

○

It's money, not love or even Newton's laws of motion, that makes the wheels go round in the Tour, as Philippe Tesnière demonstrated. A minor rider on a weak team in the late 1970s, Tesnière broke away early in a stage and stayed ahead and alone most of the day. When he was overtaken in the last few kilometers, exhausted, he slipped farther back through the pack to finish more than 7 minutes behind everybody else.

His escapade would have been remembered for no more than the weak joke it inspired—"Tesnière spent the whole race out of sight, either ahead of the pack or behind it"—until somebody thought to add up his earnings for the afternoon. They came to the franc equivalent of nearly $3,000 in those days, six years ago, when the French franc was worth twice as much against the dollar as it was in 1984. The biggest share of his prizes was a one-time-only award of 10,000 francs offered to the winner of a special sprint by a West German manufacturer of household appliances. Along his solitary way up front, Tesnière also collected 2,500 francs given to the day's overall star by a French television channel, 1,500 francs given to the day's best climber by an Italian maker of bicycle parts, and 1,000 francs given to the day's most competitive racer by a French maker of chocolate drinks.

What had made the haul especially hefty was Tesnière's status as an unemployed bicyclist, one on welfare in France. When his Fiat team had disbanded the season before, he was unable to find any employer except for the Friends of the Tour de France, a team made up entirely of French riders on welfare and underwritten by various groups as a charitable gesture. A similar team, funded by the French professional bicycle racers' union, competed in some races in 1984 although not in the Tour de France.

A few days after his breakaway, the race ended abruptly for Tesnière when he collided with a spectator, or was attacked and beaten by him, according to another version. Badly hurt, Tesnière remounted his bicycle and finished the day's run more than an hour behind the field. He was forced to withdraw from further competition and left for home with a special consolation prize of 2,500 francs to honor his spirit and dedication.

With total cash prizes twenty times greater than the Tour of Spain, for example, the Tour de France can afford such gestures. In 1984 prize money totaled 2.5 million francs (then nearly $300,000) and as always, an effort was made to spread it around. Those who finished high on a daily basis and in the overall standings were of course assured of good money, but the lesser lights could also benefit. Sometimes a prize was offered to the most competitive team, a subjective judgment that allowed room for even the weakest racers to strut their stuff. Did a rider have no hope of ever winning a day's stage? Perhaps he could still make 400 francs as the top teammate of the day. In some years, there were 500 francs available for showing the best sense of road safety, 250 francs for being judged the most elegant of the day's competitors, or 350 as the friendliest. No matter that the friendliest rider might also have been honored as the surliest, or the most elegant as the scruffiest; nobody, least of all the winners, ever quarreled with the judges.

The great bulk of the prize money was understandably carried away by the best racers: the first five finishers overall, the points champion, the best climber, the highest-ranking rider in his first Tour de France, the fastest man in time trials, the leaders of each day's stage, the man in the yellow jersey. The finishers in Paris shared 664,000 francs, with 1 million more distributed over the long haul at the rate of about 45,000 francs each day. The wearers of the yellow jersey shared 30,000 during the race; the wearers of the green, 33,000.

At the top of the final list of booty was the resort apartment valued at 120,000 francs given to the overall winner of the race, who also received 40,000 francs in cash. Second prize overall was 86,000 francs, third prize 64,000, down to 1,000 for the rider ranked eightieth. The best climber won 10,000 francs, with 70,000 more distributed during the race. Teams split nearly 200,000 francs, depending on their showings, with the best ranked in time at the end getting 25,000, and the best in points, 10,000.

On a daily basis, the winner of each stage got 2,000 francs, the second-place finisher 1,500, the third-place finisher 1,200, down to 50 francs for the riders placing fifty-first through eightieth.

Where did the money come from? Some was put up by sponsoring towns, but about two thirds came from advertisers who traveled ahead of the race, seeking business and bringing excitement to the villages where two thirds of France's 55 million people live. Life is slow out there in the villages. Official notice boards list the amusements available: domino and croquet competitions, a trout-fishing contest in a specially stocked pond, for Bastille Day fireworks and an orchestra—or at least an accordionist—and the traditional 10-franc contest to guess the weight of a pig, winner take all.

When the Tour passes through, everybody turns out, eagerly awaiting even the publicity caravan. Each piece of paper flung from a speeding car is scrutinized—the handbills about old-age annuities and furniture sales, the steelworkers' complaints about unemployment. The free samples set off a scramble for small packets of a breakfast drink, chocolate bars, balloons, and Band-Aids. Teenage girls wave at each car beseechingly, like some Cinderella hoping to flag down her prince, but the cars speed by, offering only more Band-Aids. At a café a whole family has moved chairs to the side of the road, except for the children, who are too excited to sit. The bar is deserted; the owner says, "Help yourself, pay later." Grandfather, a collapsed man wearing a tweed cap to keep off the hot sun, looks steadily up the road. His wife walks over and tucks a chocolate bar into the pocket of his shirt as he smiles his thanks.

After the free samples come the salesmen with bicycle magazines, newspaper subscriptions, and games for the children. A tethered goat bleats in a ramshackle barn. In the village square, a notice warns that all stray dogs will be picked up the morning before the Tour comes through. The local brasserie runs out of hot food as waves of visitors in press cars descend for lunch. The salesmen are still busy working from their trucks when an advance car races up, announcing the standing of the race that day and warning that the riders are heading this way.

Once the pitchmen leave, that silence descends that always announces the riders are due. Today the pack is together, and the envelope of air it generates sets the old-age annuity pamphlets tumbling in the dust. Playfully, two of the riders glide past and lift hats from the heads of spectators. The villagers run after them, laughing. This is something more than usually happens. After the bicyclists come the team cars and more press cars. Soon the road is open again; here comes a farmer with an open truck holding crates of chickens. The Tour has come and gone. Slowly, still talking about the snatched caps and the wealth of chocolate bars and breakfast drinks, everybody drifts home until next year or the one after that.

Occasionally along the route a village will offer bonus prizes to encourage action. On the La Plagne-Morzine stage, for example, Patrocinio Jimenez of the Teka team was first over the Col du Cormet de Roselend, winning a week's vacation for two at a ski resort, Pedro Delgado of the Reynolds team won 2,000 francs at the Col des Saisies, and five riders won black and white television sets at the Col de Joux-Plane. For the women in their Tour, the prizes were far smaller, such as the basket of cosmetics offered to the winner of the Douai-Béthune stage. Money almost always goes into a team pool, with merchandise —the vacation, the television sets, a wheel of cheese or country ham —kept by the individual.

Does money make a difference in a rider's performance?

The veteran manager Jean de Gribaldy told a story about his rider Joaquim Agostinho: "It was in the 1980 Bordeaux-Paris and Agostinho wanted to quit. I told him that if he hung on for one more hour, he'd get ten thousand francs for fourth place. Hearing that, he took off and began closing in on third place. So I pulled up to him again and told him that third place was worth five thousand francs more. And he finished third. You see, in cycling as in the rest of life, money talks."

For some teams in the Tour it talks faintly. Near the end of the race, Renault had collected nearly 250,000 francs in the team kitty, and Panasonic, 160,000; at the other end of the scale, the Colombians had won 22,500, and the Swiss team, Cilo-Aufina, just 14,000, which had to be split among the seven riders left in the race. But even that was a fortune compared to the earnings of Wim Myngheer of the woeful Splendor team, who finished a recent Tour 150 francs richer than he started it. Myngheer works now as a truck driver in Belgium, and his friends say he misses the cyclist's life not a bit.

○

The Tour had been drawing ever nearer Switzerland, passing through Savoie and its high meadows cut for hay, its Swiss-style chalets and their barns standing on pilings and millstones to keep climbing animals out. Today, the twentieth stage, the race crossed the border on a climb through a forest, and immediately it was plain that this was another country. The French towns leading up to the border had been clean and neat, but not so ordered. The Swiss towns were more solid somehow, more stone than wood, with more sidewalks and more parking lots than on the French side: in Switzerland, planning has gone into the growth of even villages. The roads were different too, built higher across the Alps than on the French side, crossing ridges rather than passing through valleys. They also were less rutted and patched, built deeper, and graded delicately to withstand the pushings of frost.

For all the well-being, there was a strong sense of anticlimax. In Switzerland the roads were not closed for the race until a few minutes before the riders passed, not 90 minutes in advance, the French way. In the press and official cars, it was a strange sensation, after nearly three weeks of speeding through towns and cities, to have to stop at each red light. Up ahead, where the road would have been open in France, a Dutch house trailer lurched perfectly legally ahead of the Tour. Much of the feeling of being at the center of the world disappeared when a Tour car had to wait at a crossroads because the right of way belonged to a housewife on her way to the supermarket. There was no difference for the riders, whose way was kept clear by two squads of motorcycle policemen—Swiss and the same Frenchmen who had followed them from Paris, removing only the pistols from their holsters when they passed into another sovereign state.

Again the Renault team was everywhere. On the road to Morzine, Laurent Fignon had taken a big part in the chases, like an Alpine sheepdog going after straying members of his flock. This had been regarded as a show of strength; he was saying, in effect, My team is the strongest and everybody knows it, but I don't need them to keep the pack in line. Today, on the 140-kilometer run from Morzine to Crans-Montana, he was content to let his team do most of the work. The riders to watch were the Swiss, who had won nothing so far and could be expected to play to their fans during their one day at home. Team dissension and Fignon's victories had undone them, however, and when the first breakaway began, it was a Dutchman, Henk Lubberding of the Panasonic team, who started it. Probably he hoped to win "my stage," one he might feel a right to in his eighth Tour de France.

Off with him went Pascal Jules of Renault, who had already won his stage at Nantes. They built a lead of 3 ½ minutes at the base of the final 20-kilometer climb, and Jules might have pulled away from Lubberding but hesitated to attack too early, mistaking the Dutchman's fatigue. "I overestimated him," Jules admitted. "He's so graceful that it's hard to tell when he's exhausted." While they dithered on the climb through vineyards and fields of summer vegetables, the lead elements of the pack caught up to them. Fignon was again too strong for most of the rest, jumping across the gap between the leading climbers and the two breakaways. "It was my job to go after him," Robert Millar of Peugeot said, "but I just couldn't. I was too weary by then, and he got away from us."

Six hundred meters from the finish, Fignon and Angel Arroyo were alone at the front when Fignon, standing on his pedals, found the power to pull away. He caught Arroyo in the wrong gear for acceleration, and by the time the Spaniard had sat down, changed gears, and begun rolling again, Fignon had an 11-second lead. He threw his victory bouquet into the crowd and watched with a tight smile as his fans fought for the flowers.

The Tour was finished with the Alps. In the dreaded four days, Fignon had won two stages and finished second and fifth. He led Hinault now by 9 minutes 56 seconds and the third-place LeMond by 11 minutes 9 seconds. Tapping his thighs, Hinault could say, "They betrayed me. In my head everything's all right, I feel strong. But that's not enough. There are things I can't do because my legs won't respond."

○

By now the women's race also had an apparent winner, Marianne Martin of the United States, who had taken the overall lead in the Alps by more than 3 minutes, a safe margin once the women returned to flat country. Like Fignon, she had taken the time to look around in the mountains, where she dominated the pack. "It's been gorgeous everywhere out in the country," she said, the champion as tourist. This was her first visit to France, although she had spent parts of winters skiing elsewhere in Europe. She came to bicycling by way of skiing: "I hurt my back skiing, so I took up bicycling to stay fit. That was three years ago. I did well in my first race and just kept riding. But where I really get my climber's legs is from dancing. I danced, modern and ballet, for ten years, mostly to keep active." Those years included two at Colorado State College and two at the University of Colorado, where she had been a recreation major. The twenty-six-year-old Martin had also been a white-water river guide and, until that January, a bicycle safety instructor for the city of Boulder. She quit to compete for a place on the U.S. Olympic team but finished twelfth and didn't qualify. "Everybody's lost some of their best riders to the Olympics, so we're all even," Martin said of the five national teams in the women's race. All the top women amateurs were expected for the 1985 Tour, and Martin said she welcomed the challenge. By then, she continued, she hoped to have improved her technique descending mountains. "I'm a little more cautious than I should be," she admitted. "Everybody warns you how tough the descents will be, but they really haven't been that tough. It's all in the mind."

So the Alps, as predicted, had sorted out both races, and Martin and Fignon had only to make it back to Paris without accident. "I've ridden eight Tours de France, including all of Hinault's wins, and I've never seen anyone do what Fignon's doing," Sean Kelly said. "As long as he stays healthy, he's unbeatable." In tribute, the riders turned to Fignon to appeal to the race organizers to shorten the next day's run, scheduled for 320 kilometers from Crans-Montana to Villefranche-sur-Saône, in the Beaujolais wine country. Their choice of a twenty-four-year-old rider in his second Tour as their spokesman could not be faulted. Fignon won a reduction, with the first 30 kilometers covered in team cars rather than on bicycle, disappointing only the spectators who went to the start to see the Tour de France race by.

FOURTEEN

With little at stake during the twenty-first stage, nearly ten hours on a hot and sunny road back to France, the riders decided to skylark. Vincent Barteau pretended to read a newspaper as he pedaled, and Francis Castaing did a giant crossword puzzle. Frédéric Brun of the Peugeot team turned his handlebars up, like a Sunday rider out on his three-speed, and Cyrille Guimard left his team director's car to ride along on a bicycle with the pack. The Tour de France stood on its head: Samuel Cabrera, a timid Colombian never known to mix it in sprints, was goaded into winning two for bonus points. Bernard Bourreau of Peugeot, a struggler in the mountains, was allowed to finish first in the day's opening climb. The race was decided, and everybody was heading back to Paris and then on to the critériums —Laurent Fignon was booked for more than twenty at 30,000 francs apiece—with only a few more hurdles, like the individual time trial tomorrow, and then the ceremonial passages up and down the Champs-Elysées. The war was nearly over, and all that remained for a rider was to keep his head down until the shooting stopped.

Sean Kelly did not agree, not at all. While Cabrera was playfully being allowed to win the first bonus sprint, Kelly was right behind him, gaining an 8-second reduction in his overall time. At the next bonus sprint, Kelly was again second, cutting his time by another 8 seconds. He had started the day in seventh position overall, and the 16 seconds pushed him up to fifth. Not that he was concerned about his overall standing; Kelly wanted a stage victory and was fast running out of time. He had not won a stage in the Tour in two years, a record that disappointed and even embarrassed the man ranked first among professionals after his glorious spring. Kelly is a proud man, and his desire for a stage victory was so evident that a rumor started going around that he was thinking about a possible deal with Franck Hoste of the Europ Décor team. It certainly wasn't true, those who spread the rumor said, but here's how it would work: coming up was a flying stage, an overblown bonus sprint, with points toward the green jersey given out in handfuls—35 for first place, like a stage finish on the flat, plus a 10,000-franc bonus. Hoste ranked first for the green jersey, with 246 points, or 15 ahead of Kelly, who had won the jersey the last two Tours and said he did not care if he won it again. What he wanted was "my stage." Hoste badly wanted the green jersey but did not need a stage, since he had already won two on this Tour, including the sprint in Alençon, where Kelly had been disqualified.

So, those who spread the rumor said, Kelly and Hoste would work together, with Kelly leading in Hoste, letting him ride his wheel and then, the bodyguard duty done and a lane cleared, allowing him to sprint past to victory in the flying stage and its 35 points. Then, at the end of the day in Villefranche, Hoste would lead in Kelly, clearing the lane for him and allowing Kelly to sprint past. Kelly would have "my stage" and Hoste, they said, would be so proud of his green jersey that he would probably have it bronzed.

The rumor had gotten around, and a fair number of press cars had pulled up in the town of Saint-Julien-en-Genevois for the flying stage. A sleepy place in France just across the border from Geneva, Saint-Julien had nothing much to be said for it by the Tour riders, who had been through hundreds like it before: a long, straight main street, supermarkets at both ends, a train station in the middle, and then whoosh, on to the next town. For the race organizers, Saint-Julien offered an opportunity to enliven what, on paper, promised to be a dull stage, a transition day, as the riders call it. The town fell on the time-table almost exactly between two feeding periods and two small bonus sprints, and thus could help further break up the long hours and generate some action. When the route had been laid out nine months before, who could have guessed exactly what action? asked the people fueling rumors of a Kelly-Hoste deal, winking.

Except that at the flying stage, as passengers on a milk train just in from the country cheered, Kelly was first across the line, an easy winner. The 35 points gave him the green jersey on the road.

The pack fell back into its apathy, grinding out the kilometers. In the last hour a few breakaways stepped up the pace before the day came down to a sprint into Villefranche. Kelly was at the front with such big sprinters as Hoste, Castaing, Jacques Hanegraaf, Gilbert Glaus, and even Bernard Hinault, who said he had joined in for the hell of it, to hear the wind whistle in his ears as the sprinters surged at 70 kilometers an hour. With 250 meters to go, Kelly looked back for an instant to check where Hoste was, and the Belgian passed him, not leading Kelly in but looking for victory and points toward the green jersey. Kelly decided to let Hoste go and catch him in the last 50 meters, but then, the Irishman said, the course narrowed slightly and the lane between Hanegraaf and Hoste closed as both riders shifted a bit toward the center of the road. By then, Kelly could only go wide, around them, and he didn't have a chance left of winning "my stage." He finished third, in the same time as 104 other riders, who flowed across the finish line behind Hoste, the winner of his third stage. Better, the 35 points returned the green jersey to Hoste, with 296 points to Kelly's 292.

The next day Kelly tried again during the twenty-second stage, a 51-kilometer time trial through the Beaujolais wine country. A few decades before, these hills had produced only a cheap, fruity wine known in the restaurants of Lyon to the south. Beaujolais didn't travel then because it was too small, both in quality and in production. Now, in a triumph of marketing, the short-lived young wine of Beaujolais was rushed by plane around the world for its debut each November 15. Even to Tokyo and New York, the old-timers said in wonder.

Land is everything in the new prosperity and not to be wasted in an area 55 kilometers long and 12 to 15 kilometers wide. The villages are small and tight, looking over fields left otherwise to grapes. Traveling through some villages of the Beaujolais Cru—Fleurie, Chiroubles, Morgon—and back into Villefranche, the riders finished the time trial quickly. With only Fignon still out on the road, Kelly led the field in 1 hour 7 minutes 19 seconds. Hinault was second, 36 seconds behind, and Greg LeMond was third, 41 seconds behind. For three days LeMond had not been able to gain time on Hinault in their battle for second place overall. He had done no better today, even though Hinault had lost 20 seconds with a flat tire. Fignon was having his troubles too, as his chain rattled loose and he had to change bicycles. With a long sprint, he finished in the same clocking as Kelly before the timers broke it down to thousandths of a second: Kelly 263 and Fignon 215, not quite a twentieth of a second faster.

A shocked Kelly could do no more than mutter obscenities as Fignon hurried over to say that he had ridden his race, not kept the time. Kelly was not to be comforted, even though the 8 points he got for second place put him at 300, or 4 better than Hoste for the green jersey.

○

To hear him tell it, Bernard Tapie had all the answers, because it was his job to have all the answers. At age forty he was a symbol of the new entrepreneurial spirit France needed, the working-class boy who had grown rich while the country grappled with huge trade deficits, high unemployment, and inflation. As bankruptcies increased—nearing 25,000 a year, an annual increase of 10 percent—Tapie had made a fortune by buying failed companies, reorganizing them, and nursing them back to profitability. The forty companies he owned or controlled reported $500 million in annual sales. He estimated his own assets at more than $100 million, and he was happy to give away his secrets in *L'Equipe.*

"In a time like this for France, with our economic problems, a lack of discipline, ambition, and courage, we ought to invite the big bosses to watch some daily stages of the Tour rather than go off to business seminars. Here they might get a chance to learn some lessons about efficiency.

"I'm speaking about fighting spirit. The best businessmen and the top athletes are motivated by the same taste for victory. Only results make a champion. In sports you learn to measure yourself by attaining your goals. It's a good lesson for businessmen. Money and glory are something extra for a champion, and I think that's true too in business. If you start a business simply to make money, you've got a 99 percent chance of failing. Money is the way to measure success or failure, not success itself."

Tapie said he was happy to spend 10 million francs (then a bit more than $1 million) a year on the Vie Claire bicycle team, calling it a good investment. His La Vie Claire health-food stores had benefited from their new identification with Bernard Hinault and so had the co-sponsors, Terraillon scales and Look sports equipment, which was working with Hinault to develop a better toe clip for bicyclists. Both were Tapie properties. So was the Mic-Mac company, which produced the team's red, white, and yellow jerseys in a pattern modeled on a Mondrian painting. The jerseys had been joked about when they appeared; yet, Tapie said, already 35,000 had been sold to fans in bicycle shops.

Tapie said that Hinault had given a cachet to his companies, that his workers liked to identify with a champion: "It's important for a worker to be proud of the company that employs him. Nobody goes around shouting from the rooftops that he works for a company with a bad name. Psychologically it's important to work for a company that's successful." La Vie Claire had been successful in this Tour, and so bicycling had been a good investment.

But Tapie had some problems with his new world. Months before, in another interview with *L'Equipe,* he had used a phrase that had been thrown back in his face many times since. "The sport," he said, "is in the Middle Ages." Even if his words were exaggerated, he could make a case. "The professional rider is treated like the lowest worker thirty years ago. When he doesn't have it anymore, a team just drops him. Even a bookkeeper is better protected, because he has a union behind him. If you're talking about human and social relations, you'd have to go back a century to find anything similar." His team, he boasted, would provide jobs in Tapie's many industries when a rider was through.

"Today's bosses have to take account of their partnership with their workers, unionized or not. The times are gone when you inspired people with nothing more than a slap on the back. Paternalism is finished. We're beyond the days when a manager's conversation with his riders was, 'Okay, kid, off you go.' He gave him a pat on the bottom and that was that. To communicate, you have to do better than that."

Then there is the problem of continuity. "Two months from the end of the season, and still nobody knows how many teams will continue next year," he noted. "It's the law of silence, of permanent suspicion, including the whole subject of drugs. A victory must always be greeted with suspicion. The rules of the game aren't very clear."

One rule he did not like—even while his companies benefited from it—was team sponsorship, and he mocked firms that sponsored athletes solely as a means of publicity. Tapie kept urging a return of national and regional teams in the Tour, a concept abandoned since 1968. "The whole world must become interested in the race," he insisted. "It has to become something really international, like the Olympic Games. We've got to go outside France. One year in France, the next in Italy, Spain, or Colombia. We've got to take the race to the public out there."

Tapie admitted that he had met strong resistance to his ideas for racing. "I like what other people call impossible missions. If you want people to notice you, do something spectacular. What impact would it have if I took over a company in good financial shape? It's the same thing in bicycling. What would it have meant to hire Hinault when he was at his peak? The first time I met him, I asked him about his knee, and he answered, 'There's just one chance in two that I'll ride again.' That made me want to do everything I could to give him his chance."

Hinault had become a close friend, Tapie said, signed to a ten-year personal-services contract with a handsome share of stock. Hinault's success in the Tour pleased Tapie. "We would have failed if people were whistling and booing Hinault during the race. But I tell you, he's never been so well-liked by the public. His popularity will translate into business for our companies, but that's not why I'm so pleased for him. He's made so much progress in communicating. He's become more accessible, more sensitive, and he's done himself only good by the way he's accepted his challenges."

Not many people trooped into the small room in Villefranche-sur-Saône after the time trial when Hinault held his last press conference, but Tapie was there. He listened carefully while his rider, encouraging questions, defended his strategy during the race.

"I attacked and kept attacking," Hinault said. "Often somebody else wins, and this time somebody else did. That's life and that's racing." He praised Laurent Fignon as "a great rider who has exploded," adding, "This year I ran into a super Fignon. Next year, who knows?"

There would be a next year for him in the Tour. "I hope to win in 1985," Hinault announced shortly after saying that he intended to become merely a road captain for younger riders. "We're going to recruit younger riders," he said. Sliding off a question about luring away Greg

LeMond, he said, "A man who works for another has to make a choice. For the moment, he's chosen Renault."

Intense and charming, Hinault leaned forward and gave his final verdict: "No doubt I made the mistake of wanting to win at any price. But what do you want? I can't change at my age." He had finished second among 170 riders who nearly a month before had started the world's most important bicycle race. If this consoled him, he did not mention it. Second place was for others, but he seemed relaxed and patient.

"I'm proud of him," Tapie said at the other end of the room. "He's learned a lot, hasn't he?" At that moment, Tapie, not Hinault, seemed the man in need of consolation.

○

Triumphantly by special train to Paris, where Gilbert Glaus, *la lanterne rouge,* could say, "Last? I don't look at it that way. I'll be in Paris with a hundred and twenty others. Last among them, maybe, but ahead of fifty who quit. I'm there, there, I've suffered to be there."

There was no hope in this twenty-third stage that Glaus could catch the next-to-last rider, Manuel Russenberger, his Cilo-Aufina teammate, who was nearly 2 minutes ahead of him, but the day did offer one last chance at a stage victory. As Glaus liked to remind people, he had won on the Champs-Elysées just the year before, so why not again? It was also the last chance for the man Glaus had beaten in the sprint the year before, Sean Kelly. And for Franck Hoste, who had to finish today in the first five and beat Kelly in order to collect enough points to retake the green jersey. For Greg LeMond there was no hope of catching Bernard Hinault, 1 minute 14 seconds ahead in second place, short of a disabling crash. For Hinault even a crash might not be enough to stop Laurent Fignon, 10 minutes 32 seconds ahead; with the final victory in sight, riders stay in the race even with broken collarbones or arms.

Not that riders have not won the Tour on the last day. It happened most recently in 1968, when Jan Janssen finished first in a time trial and snatched victory by 38 seconds in a Tour in which he never wore the yellow jersey until he put it on just before everybody at last went home. Most years, however, the point was to tie up loose ends or see if some rider would break away on the Champs-Elysées, where many had tried and had always been brought back to the pack before its sprint finish.

The crowds began arriving early, knowing that the avenue would be jammed from the Tuileries to the Arc de Triomphe, a stretch that the riders would pass six times at the end of a 196-kilometer trip from the suburbs. Paris was the traditional finish of the Tour, but the Champs-Elysées had been the final lap only since 1975, when the organizers persuaded a reluctant government to close the avenue to car traffic for most of the day. Before that, the race had ended in either the Parc des Princes stadium or the Cipale velodrome in Vincennes, but neither could attract the half million spectators that the Champs-Elysées would. Extra tables were being set out at most of the cafés, and the souvenir salesmen were busy. Nearby, the outdoor stamp market was just closing. On a soft summer's day, with a breeze fluttering the French flags along the avenue, the thronged finish was the last piece of folklore.

First came the women, with Marianne Martin comfortable in her lead of 3 minutes 17 seconds. She finished in the middle of the pack, taking no part in the bonus sprints along the avenue, careful to keep teammates around her for protection. Second overall was Heleen Hage of the Netherlands, with Deborah Shumway of the United States third, Valérie Simmonet of France fourth, and Corinne Lutz of France fifth. Martin easily won the mountain climber's jersey and the United States won the team title. The overall elapsed time for Martin was 29 hours 39 minutes 2 seconds.

The men arrived a few hours later at the end of an uneventful afternoon. When they reached the Champs-Elysées, Alain Bondue of La Redoute set off on what was to be the final breakaway, leading the pack on nearly five circuits of the avenue. He was hauled in on the fifth and then the riders began their final 6 kilometers, slightly uphill toward the Arc de Triomphe, a last sweep in front of that monument, slightly downhill toward and around the Tuileries, through the Place de la Concorde in one last echelon and up toward the finish line, where the loudspeakers were screaming their names.

With a kilometer to go, Fignon surged forward, trying to lead in his teammate Pascal Jules. They had the power, but it was a time for raw speed, the sprinter's art. Eric Vanderaerden of Panasonic overtook them in the last 250 meters and easily passed Jules, hurling his arms upward in the ultimate stage victory. As Fignon dropped back, Hoste drove by him for third place and the points he needed to win the green jersey. Kelly finished fifth, behind Hinault, but even fourth place would not have been enough. The pack was across, the last man Bondue.

"A very hard Tour," Hinault called it earlier. "This wasn't a Tour just for climbers," Marc Durant of the Système U team said, "but for strong men." His judgment was confirmed by the figures: 124 finished what 170 started, with Fignon recording the best overall elapsed time of 112 hours 3 minutes 40 seconds. Next in the final general classification were Hinault, second; LeMond, third; Millar, fourth; Kelly, fifth; Angel Arroyo, sixth; Pascal Simon, seventh; Pedro Munoz, eighth; Claude Criquielion, ninth; and Phil Anderson, tenth. Luis Herrera, the Colombian climber, was twenty-seventh, and Vincent Barteau, the man in the yellow jersey for two weeks, twenty-eighth. Millar won the polka-dot jersey as king of the mountains, and LeMond the white one for the highest-ranked neophyte. A few of the riders shook hands and then rolled their bicycles toward their team cars and mechanics. It was over.

As Fignon, Hinault, and LeMond were led up the steps to the victory podium, the crowds began to chant the Frenchmen's names. "Feen-yon, Feen-yon," they called out, and he waved back in joy. "I like real popularity rather than celebrity," he had said. "But my ambition is simply to win a lot of races and make a lot of money. I'm not ashamed to admit that I ride for glory and money. They go together." As he lifted the Sèvres porcelain vase that goes to the winner, the crowd chanted his name again. "Nothing explains his progress in the last 12 months," Jacques Anquetil wrote. "Never in the history of bicycling has a rider made so much progress in so little time. He's able to win on any ground and now he adds panache. He could have played it safe, but he'd rather take some risks for glory. There's no superlative strong enough when you talk about him. Fignon is a phenomenon."

"Ee-no, Ee-no," the crowds were chanting now. "I'm not really surprised by my new popularity," Hinault had said at L'Alpe-d'Huez. "They consider me weaker than Fignon this time, and so I get more sympathy." He waved at the crowd once, twice, then retreated, careful not to stand in front of Fignon. "I don't believe Hinault is suddenly old," his longtime teammate Alain Vigneron had said. "If you think Hinault can't win next year, he's going to surprise you. He'll be stronger next year."

And finally Raymond Poulidor, who knew more about second place in the Tour de France than a man needed to know: "Hinault was Fignon's only opponent. Without Fignon, Hinault was the winner. If you blame Hinault for making mistakes, it was Fignon's domination that forced him to make them. Hinault was right to say second place didn't interest him. And in going for it all, he sewed up second."

In the crowd, somebody held up a sign with words the riders had been seeing for days along the route. "Bravo Fignon, Merci Hinault," it said, and everybody had a chance to read it one last time. The joyful Fignon waved again and again to his fans. Appetite, the French say, comes from eating.

○

A few weeks later, early in September, Greg LeMond was strongly denying published reports that he had jumped teams and signed a $1 million contract with La Vie Claire for the next three years. "I haven't signed anything," he said over the telephone from his home in Belgium. "We've done a lot of talking but it's not certain yet that I'll be leaving Renault." La Vie Claire had announced the day before that LeMond had signed with it for the 1985 season, abrogating his contract with Renault. Bernard Tapie said it was up to LeMond "to free himself of his other commitments."

LeMond insisted that he was still negotiating to stay with Renault. "I'd like to stay with Renault," he said. "If I knew Renault was going to sign me for three more years with the same kind of deal Tapie has offered, I'd sign with them. But if things can't work out with Renault, I'll go with Tapie." He confirmed that Tapie had offered a minimum of $1 million over three years, a good jump from LeMond's Renault salary, which was estimated at $200,000 a year—payable in dollars— plus such bonuses as the rent on his house, company cars and eight round-trip plane tickets a year to the United States for him and his wife. His annual income was believed to be $500,000, including money from the 30 to 40 critériums he rode each season and endorsement fees —the center of his troubles with Renault, he said. "They've let several

companies abuse my name," he complained. "There are five companies I've got lawsuits going against because they say I've endorsed
their products—brakes, saddles, all the components. Renault promised
they'd help me fight this, but they haven't done a thing.

"They don't want to talk about my future," LeMond complained of
Renault. "It's a firm offer from Tapie, and it kind of secures my future."
(And, Tapie hoped, that of his sportswear and health-food stores in the
U.S. market. "If he weren't an American," Tapie said of LeMond and
his $1 million contract, "there would be a zero less.") LeMond said he
expected no legal problems in breaking his contract. "We really don't
have a formal contract," he continued. "I've had my lawyers look at
what we do have, and they say there won't be any problem since it's
so one-sided. Besides, no team really wants to keep a rider who doesn't
want to ride for it. It winds up with everybody unhappy. When Hinault
left, he still had four years to go on his contract, but they let him out
of it."

LeMond denied that his possible switch to La Vie Claire reflected
any unhappiness with his teammates, especially Laurent Fignon.
"Fignon and I are good friends," he insisted. "It's the best team in the
world, and Cyrille Guimard is the best coach in the world. I've got a
lot of friends there, but the way La Vie Claire is building itself up, it
may be the second-best team around." Since the Tour, La Vie Claire
had signed Steve Bauer, a Canadian who had finished second in the
Olympic Games road race and third in the professional world championship, and Kim Andersen, the Danish leader of the Peugeot team,
which had disbanded.

Peugeot was not the only victim of its poor showing in the Tour.
Système U and Europ Décor also folded, and La Redoute, Teka, and
Cilo-Aufina changed managers. Fignon and Hinault dropped out in the
world championship as LeMond finished twenty-seventh and lost his
rainbow jersey to Claude Criquielion, a Belgian who had finished an
anonymous ninth in the Tour but now was celebrated as perhaps the
new Eddy Merckx. Fons De Wolf moved to a French team, and Franck
Hoste to an Italian one. Hinault won two fall classics: the prestigious
Grand Prix de Nations and the Tour of Lombardy. "What do they say
now?" he asked, "all those who said I was finished?"

The season wound down. LeMond finally did sign with La Vie

Claire, and Sean Kelly collected a trophy and $5,000 for winning the Super Prestige Pernod competition as the season's top-ranked professional bicyclist. Vincent Barteau rode a few six-day races—which are to road racing what boil-in-the-bag beef stew is to *boeuf bourguignon* —because, he said, "The public wants to see Barteau. Now they all know who I am." On tropical Réunion Island, Joop Zoetemelk rode to victory in a small race.

France's economy got no better, and soup kitchens opened in Paris. "The new poor," a class that would probably never find work again, were discovered by the press. Hoping to attract more money, the International Cycling Union relaxed its rules to permit the names of sponsors to be placed nearly anywhere on a rider's uniform. Coca-Cola outbid Perrier for the contract it had held for fifty years as the Tour's official drink, available free to all finishers of each day's ride. As the organizers so dearly wished, the Tour de France grew increasingly international. Following Panasonic's lead, other Japanese companies began sponsoring European teams: Hitachi joined Splendor, Yoko joined Kwantum, and Nissan joined the new Verandalux team. Soon it was winter again and the bicycling magazines had little to publish besides the classic photograph of professional racing: in soft focus in the foreground a field of poppies or bachelor's buttons or daffodils, and behind the flowers the riders in their short-sleeved jerseys. From the relaxed way they sat on their bicycles, it was obvious that the road ahead was empty, that the race was under control, and that nobody was off on a breakaway.

Appendix

LEADERS AFTER THE PROLOGUE

From Montreuil-sous-Bois to Noisy-le-Sec

		Total Elapsed Time
1.	Bernard Hinault	6 minutes 39 seconds
2.	Laurent Fignon	3 seconds behind
3.	Allan Peiper	9 seconds behind
4.	Phil Anderson	9 seconds behind
5.	Sean Yates	10 seconds behind
6.	Jean-Luc Vandenbroucke	11 seconds behind
7.	Stephen Roche	12 seconds behind
8.	Joop Zoetemelk	12 seconds behind
9.	Greg LeMond	12 seconds behind
10.	Gerrie Knetemann	14 seconds behind
11.	Alain Bondue	14 seconds behind

LEADERS AFTER THE FIRST STAGE

Bondy–Saint-Denis

		Total Elapsed Time
1.	Ludo Peeters	3 hours 33 minutes 48 seconds
2.	Franck Hoste	4 seconds behind
3.	Allan Peiper	8 seconds behind
4.	Bernard Hinault	8 seconds behind
5.	Jacques Hanegraaf	11 seconds behind
6.	Laurent Fignon	12 seconds behind
7.	Phil Anderson	18 seconds behind
8.	Sean Yates	19 seconds behind
9.	Jean-Luc Vandenbroucke	20 seconds behind
10.	Stephen Roche	21 seconds behind
11.	Joop Zoetemelk	21 seconds behind
12.	Greg LeMond	21 seconds behind

LEADERS AFTER THE SECOND STAGE

Bobigny–Louvroil

		Total Elapsed Time
1.	Jacques Hanegraaf	10 hours 34 minutes 17 seconds
2.	Adri Van der Poel	1 second behind
3.	Kim Andersen	8 seconds behind
4.	Marc Madiot	8 seconds behind
5.	Jean-Luc Vandenbroucke	9 seconds behind
6.	Ludo Peeters	9 seconds behind
7.	Allan Peiper	13 seconds behind
8.	Franck Hoste	13 seconds behind
9.	Greg LeMond	14 seconds behind
10.	Phil Anderson	15 seconds behind

LEADERS AFTER THE THIRD STAGE

Louvroil–Valenciennes

		Total Elapsed Time
1.	Jacques Hanegraaf	11 hours 38 minutes 15 seconds
2.	Adri Van der Poel	1 second behind
3.	Marc Madiot	3 seconds behind
4.	Ludo Peeters	9 seconds behind
5.	Greg LeMond	10 seconds behind
6.	Laurent Fignon	13 seconds behind
7.	Phil Anderson	15 seconds behind
8.	Eric Vanderaerden	23 seconds behind
9.	Joop Zoetemelk	30 seconds behind
10.	Pascal Jules	33 seconds behind

LEADERS AFTER THE FOURTH STAGE

Valenciennes–Béthune

		Total Elapsed Time
1.	Adri Van der Poel	13 hours 58 minutes 11 seconds
2.	Phil Anderson	8 seconds behind
3.	Jacques Hanegraaf	9 seconds behind
4.	Marc Madiot	13 seconds behind
5.	Ludo Peeters	18 seconds behind
6.	Greg LeMond	19 seconds behind
7.	Laurent Fignon	22 seconds behind
8.	Eric Vanderaerden	32 seconds behind
9.	Joop Zoetemelk	39 seconds behind
10.	Pascal Jules	42 seconds behind

Leaders after the Fifth Stage

Béthune–Cergy-Pontoise

		Total Elapsed Time
1.	Vincent Barteau	18 hours 47 minutes 53 seconds
2.	Maurice Le Guilloux	1 minute 33 seconds behind
3.	Paulo Ferreira	3 minutes 13 seconds behind
4.	Adri Van der Poel	17 minutes 45 seconds behind
5.	Phil Anderson	17 minutes 53 seconds behind
6.	Jacques Hanegraaf	17 minutes 54 seconds behind
7.	Marc Madiot	17 minutes 58 seconds behind
8.	Ludo Peeters	18 minutes 3 seconds behind
9.	Greg LeMond	18 minutes 4 seconds behind
10.	Laurent Fignon	18 minutes 7 seconds behind

Leaders after the Sixth Stage

Cergy-Pontoise–Alençon

		Total Elapsed Time
1.	Vincent Barteau	24 hours 2 minutes 58 seconds
2.	Maurice Le Guilloux	1 minute 41 seconds behind
3.	Paulo Ferreira	3 minutes 13 seconds behind
4.	Phil Anderson	17 minutes 33 seconds behind
5.	Adri Van der Poel	17 minutes 53 seconds behind
6.	Eric Vanderaerden	17 minutes 55 seconds behind
7.	Jacques Hanegraaf	18 minutes 2 seconds behind
8.	Marc Madiot	18 minutes 6 seconds behind
9.	Ludo Peeters	18 minutes 11 seconds behind
10.	Laurent Fignon	18 minutes 11 seconds behind

Leaders after the Seventh Stage

Alençon–Le Mans

		Total Elapsed Time
1.	Vincent Barteau	25 hours 35 minutes 48 seconds
2.	Maurice Le Guilloux	3 minutes 7 seconds behind
3.	Paulo Ferreira	9 minutes 57 seconds behind
4.	Laurent Fignon	12 minutes 54 seconds behind
5.	Phil Anderson	13 minutes 40 seconds behind
6.	Bernard Hinault	14 minutes 23 seconds behind
7.	Gerard Veldscholten	14 minutes 33 seconds behind
8.	Greg LeMond	15 minutes 3 seconds behind
9.	Roberto Visentini	15 minutes 41 seconds behind
10.	Stephen Roche	15 minutes 45 seconds behind

Leaders after the Eighth Stage

Le Mans–Nantes

		Total Elapsed Time
1.	Vincent Barteau	29 hours 54 minutes 58 seconds
2.	Maurice Le Guilloux	3 minutes 7 seconds behind
3.	Paulo Ferreira	9 minutes 57 seconds behind
4.	Laurent Fignon	12 minutes 42 seconds behind
5.	Phil Anderson	13 minutes 40 seconds behind
6.	Bernard Hinault	14 minutes 23 seconds behind
7.	Gerard Veldscholten	14 minutes 33 seconds behind
8.	Greg LeMond	15 minutes 3 seconds behind
9.	Ludo Peeters	15 minutes 19 seconds behind
10.	Kim Andersen	15 minutes 39 seconds behind

LEADERS AFTER THE NINTH STAGE

Nantes–Bordeaux

		Total Elapsed Time
1.	Vincent Barteau	39 hours 35 minutes 14 seconds
2.	Maurice Le Guilloux	3 minutes 7 seconds behind
3.	Paulo Ferreira	9 minutes 57 seconds behind
4.	Laurent Fignon	12 minutes 30 seconds behind
5.	Phil Anderson	13 minutes 28 seconds behind
6.	Bernard Hinault	13 minutes 43 seconds behind
7.	Gerard Veldscholten	14 minutes 33 seconds behind
8.	Greg LeMond	15 minutes 3 seconds behind
9.	Ludo Peeters	15 minutes 19 seconds behind
10.	Kim Andersen	15 minutes 39 seconds behind

LEADERS AFTER THE TENTH STAGE

Bordeaux–Pau

		Total Elapsed Time
1.	Vincent Barteau	44 hours 28 minutes 47 seconds
2.	Maurice Le Guilloux	3 minutes 7 seconds behind
3.	Laurent Fignon	12 minutes 30 seconds behind
4.	Paulo Ferreira	13 minutes 19 seconds behind
5.	Phil Anderson	13 minutes 38 seconds behind
6.	Bernard Hinault	13 minutes 43 seconds behind
7.	Gerard Veldscholten	14 minutes 33 seconds behind
8.	Greg LeMond	15 minutes 3 seconds behind
9.	Ludo Peeters	15 minutes 19 seconds behind
10.	Sean Kelly	15 minutes 36 seconds behind

LEADERS AFTER THE ELEVENTH STAGE

Pau–Guzet-Neige

		Total Elapsed Time
1.	Vincent Barteau	51 hours 36 minutes 38 seconds
2.	Maurice Le Guilloux	7 minutes 37 seconds behind
3.	Laurent Fignon	10 minutes 33 seconds behind
4.	Gerard Veldscholten	12 minutes 28 seconds behind
5.	Bernard Hinault	12 minutes 38 seconds behind
6.	Phil Anderson	13 minutes 29 seconds behind
7.	Robert Millar	14 minutes 24 seconds behind
8.	Sean Kelly	14 minutes 31 seconds behind
9.	Greg LeMond	14 minutes 35 seconds behind
10.	Pedro Delgado	14 minutes 37 seconds behind

LEADERS AFTER THE TWELFTH STAGE

Saint Girons–Blagnac

		Total Elapsed Time
1.	Vincent Barteau	54 hours 17 minutes 18 seconds
2.	Maurice Le Guilloux	7 minutes 47 seconds behind
3.	Laurent Fignon	10 minutes 25 seconds behind
4.	Gerard Veldscholten	12 minutes 28 seconds behind
5.	Bernard Hinault	12 minutes 38 seconds behind
6.	Phil Anderson	13 minutes 29 seconds behind
7.	Greg LeMond	14 minutes 23 seconds behind
8.	Sean Kelly	14 minutes 31 seconds behind
9.	Pedro Delgado	14 minutes 37 seconds behind
10.	Robert Millar	14 minutes 47 seconds behind

LEADERS AFTER THE THIRTEENTH STAGE

Blagnac–Rodez

		Total Elapsed Time
1.	Vincent Barteau	60 hours 27 minutes 39 seconds
2.	Maurice Le Guilloux	8 minutes 7 seconds behind
3.	Laurent Fignon	10 minutes 25 seconds behind
4.	Gerard Veldscholten	12 minutes 28 seconds behind
5.	Bernard Hinault	12 minutes 38 seconds behind
6.	Phil Anderson	13 minutes 29 seconds behind
7.	Pierre-Henri Menthéour	14 minutes 18 seconds behind
8.	Greg LeMond	14 minutes 23 seconds behind
9.	Sean Kelly	14 minutes 31 seconds behind
10.	Pedro Delgado	14 minutes 37 seconds behind

LEADERS AFTER THE FOURTEENTH STAGE

Rodez–Domaine du Rouret

		Total Elapsed Time
1.	Vincent Barteau	66 hours 46 minutes 16 seconds
2.	Maurice Le Guilloux	8 minutes 7 seconds behind
3.	Laurent Fignon	10 minutes 13 seconds behind
4.	Fons De Wolf	11 minutes 42 seconds behind
5.	Bernard Hinault	12 minutes 26 seconds behind
6.	Gerard Veldscholten	12 minutes 28 seconds behind
7.	Phil Anderson	13 minutes 17 seconds behind
8.	Greg LeMond	14 minutes 23 seconds behind
9.	Sean Kelly	14 minutes 27 seconds behind
10.	Pedro Delgado	14 minutes 37 seconds behind

LEADERS AFTER THE FIFTEENTH STAGE

Domaine du Rouret–Grenoble

Total Elapsed Time

1. Vincent Barteau   73 hours 52 minutes 19 seconds
2. Laurent Fignon   10 minutes 13 seconds behind
3. Bernard Hinault   12 minutes 26 seconds behind
4. Gerard Veldscholten   12 minutes 28 seconds behind
5. Phil Anderson   13 minutes 17 seconds behind
6. Greg LeMond   14 minutes 23 seconds behind
7. Sean Kelly   14 minutes 27 seconds behind
8. Pedro Delgado   14 minutes 37 seconds behind
9. Robert Millar   14 minutes 56 seconds behind
10. Peter Winnen   16 minutes 42 seconds behind

LEADERS AFTER THE SIXTEENTH STAGE

Les Echelles–La Ruchère

Total Elapsed Time

1. Vincent Barteau   74 hours 38 minutes 14 seconds
2. Laurent Fignon   6 minutes 29 seconds behind
3. Bernard Hinault   9 minutes 15 seconds behind
4. Phil Anderson   11 minutes 3 seconds behind
5. Gerard Veldscholten   11 minutes 16 seconds behind
6. Pedro Delgado   11 minutes 25 seconds behind
7. Sean Kelly   12 minutes 4 seconds behind
8. Greg LeMond   12 minutes 33 seconds behind
9. Robert Millar   12 minutes 50 seconds behind
10. Angel Arroyo   14 minutes 31 seconds behind

Leaders after the Seventeenth Stage

Grenoble–L'Alpe-d'Huez

		Total Elapsed Time
1.	Laurent Fignon	79 hours 24 minutes 56 seconds
2.	Vincent Barteau	4 minutes 22 seconds behind
3.	Bernard Hinault	5 minutes 41 seconds behind
4.	Robert Millar	8 minutes 25 seconds behind
5.	Greg LeMond	8 minutes 45 seconds behind
6.	Gerard Veldscholten	9 minutes 3 seconds behind
7.	Angel Arroyo	9 minutes 40 seconds behind
8.	Phil Anderson	11 minutes 9 seconds behind
9.	Luis Herrera	11 minutes 12 seconds behind
10.	Pedro Delgado	13 minutes 13 seconds behind

Leaders after the Eighteenth Stage

L'Alpe-d'Huez–La Plagne

		Total Elapsed Time
1.	Laurent Fignon	85 hours 37 minutes 41 seconds
2.	Bernard Hinault	8 minutes 39 seconds behind
3.	Greg LeMond	9 minutes 52 seconds behind
4.	Robert Millar	10 minutes 9 seconds behind
5.	Pedro Delgado	14 minutes 40 seconds behind
6.	Pascal Simon	15 minutes 45 seconds behind
7.	Sean Kelly	16 minutes 31 seconds behind
8.	Angel Arroyo	18 minutes 12 seconds behind
9.	Niki Ruttimann	21 minutes 4 seconds behind
10.	Claude Criquielion	21 minutes 7 seconds behind

Leaders after the Nineteenth Stage

La Plagne–Morzine

Total Elapsed Time

1. Laurent Fignon   91 hours 55 minutes 20 seconds
2. Bernard Hinault   8 minutes 39 seconds behind
3. Greg LeMond   9 minutes 52 seconds behind
4. Robert Millar   10 minutes 16 seconds behind
5. Pascal Simon   15 minutes 45 seconds behind
6. Sean Kelly   16 minutes 21 seconds behind
7. Angel Arroyo   16 minutes 58 seconds behind
8. Pedro Delgado   17 minutes 37 seconds behind
9. Pedro Munoz   21 minutes 11 seconds behind
10. Niki Ruttimann   22 minutes 54 seconds behind

Leaders after the Twentieth Stage

Morzine–Crans-Montana

Total Elapsed Time

1. Laurent Fignon   96 hours 4 minutes 36 seconds
2. Bernard Hinault   9 minutes 56 seconds behind
3. Greg LeMond   11 minutes 9 seconds behind
4. Robert Millar   11 minutes 49 seconds behind
5. Pascal Simon   16 minutes 55 seconds behind
6. Angel Arroyo   17 minutes 9 seconds behind
7. Sean Kelly   17 minutes 31 seconds behind
8. Pedro Munoz   22 minutes 18 seconds behind
9. Claude Criquielion   25 minutes 12 seconds behind
10. Niki Ruttimann   26 minutes 28 seconds behind

Leaders after the Twenty-first Stage

Crans-Montana–Villefranche-sur-Saône

Total Elapsed Time

1. Laurent Fignon   105 hours 32 minutes 44 seconds
2. Bernard Hinault   9 minutes 56 seconds behind
3. Greg LeMond   11 minutes 5 seconds behind
4. Robert Millar   11 minutes 45 seconds behind
5. Sean Kelly   16 minutes 35 seconds behind
6. Pascal Simon   16 minutes 51 seconds behind
7. Angel Arroyo   17 minutes 5 seconds behind
8. Pedro Munoz   22 minutes 18 seconds behind
9. Claude Criquielion   25 minutes 12 seconds behind
10. Niki Ruttimann   26 minutes 28 seconds behind

Leaders after the Twenty-second Stage

Villié Morgon–Villefranche-sur-Saône

Total Elapsed Time

1. Laurent Fignon   106 hours 40 minutes 3 seconds
2. Bernard Hinault   10 minutes 32 seconds behind
3. Greg LeMond   11 minutes 46 seconds behind
4. Robert Millar   14 minutes 42 seconds behind
5. Sean Kelly   16 minutes 35 seconds behind
6. Angel Arroyo   19 minutes 22 seconds behind
7. Pascal Simon   21 minutes 17 seconds behind
8. Pedro Munoz   26 minutes 17 seconds behind
9. Claude Criquielion   29 minutes 12 seconds behind
10. Phil Anderson   29 minutes 16 seconds behind

FINAL OVERALL STANDINGS

		Team	Total Elapsed Time
1.	Fignon	(Ren)	112 hours 3 minutes 40 seconds
2.	Hinault	(VC)	10 minutes 32 seconds behind
3.	LeMond	(Ren)	11 minutes 46 seconds behind
4.	Millar	(Peu)	14 minutes 42 seconds behind
5.	Kelly	(Ski)	16 minutes 35 seconds behind
6.	Arroyo	(Rey)	19 minutes 22 seconds behind
7.	Pascal Simon	(Peu)	21 minutes 17 seconds behind
8.	Munoz	(Tek)	26 minutes 17 seconds behind
9.	Criquielion	(Spl)	29 minutes 12 seconds behind
10.	Anderson	(Pan)	29 minutes 16 seconds behind
11.	Ruttimann	(VC)	30 minutes 58 seconds behind
12.	Acevedo	(Col)	33 minutes 32 seconds behind
13.	Grézet	(Ski)	33 minutes 41 seconds behind
14.	Caritoux	(Ski)	36 minutes 28 seconds behind
15.	Jiminez	(Tek)	37 minutes 49 seconds behind
16.	Veldscholten	(Pan)	41 minutes 54 seconds behind
17.	Laurent	(Cop)	44 minutes 33 seconds behind
18.	Florez	(Col)	45 minutes 33 seconds behind
19.	Agudelo	(Col)	49 minutes 25 seconds behind
20.	Gavillet	(Cil)	51 minutes 2 seconds behind
21.	Jules	(Ren)	51 minutes 53 seconds behind
22.	Loro	(Car)	52 minutes 37 seconds behind
23.	Vichot	(Ski)	53 minutes 18 seconds behind
24.	Nulens	(Pan)	53 minutes 25 seconds behind
25.	Roche	(Red)	56 minutes 36 seconds behind
26.	Winnen	(Pan)	58 minutes 14 seconds behind
27.	Herrera	(Col)	58 minutes 30 seconds behind
28.	Barteau	(Ren)	1h 0 minutes 2 seconds behind
29.	Mas	(Ski)	1h 5 minutes 38 seconds behind
30.	Zoetemelk	(Kwa)	1h 6 minutes 2 seconds behind
31.	Boyer	(Ski)	1h 7 minutes 3 seconds behind
32.	Cabrera	(Col)	1h 7 minutes 17 seconds behind
33.	Garde	(Peu)	1h 9 minutes 58 seconds behind
34.	Prieto	(Rey)	1h 10 minutes 23 seconds behind

35. Marc Madiot	(Rey)	1h 13 minutes 3 seconds behind
36. Jérome Simon	(Red)	1h 16 minutes 33 seconds behind
37. Durant	(Sys)	1h 17 minutes 22 seconds behind
38. Alban	(Red)	1h 18 minutes 3 seconds behind
39. Echave	(Tek)	1h 22 minutes 59 seconds behind
40. Lubberding	(Pan)	1h 23 minutes 52 seconds behind
41. Lagula	(Rey)	1h 24 minutes 2 seconds behind
42. Van Den Brande	(Spl)	1h 24 minutes 13 seconds behind
43. Breu	(Cil)	1h 25 minutes 21 seconds behind
44. Le Bigaut	(Cop)	1h 26 minutes 51 seconds behind
45. Rodriguez	(Spl)	1h 28 minutes 35 seconds behind
46. Yvon Madiot	(Ren)	1h 29 minutes 39 seconds behind
47. Vigneron	(VC)	1h 29 minutes 49 seconds behind
48. Sergeant	(Eur)	1h 31 minutes 13 seconds behind
49. Bérard	(VC)	1h 33 minutes 15 seconds behind
50. Andersen	(Cop)	1h 33 minutes 23 seconds behind
51. Aja	(Rey)	1h 33 minutes 53 seconds behind
52. Gorospe	(Rey)	1h 37 minutes 23 seconds behind
53. Hernandez	(Rey)	1h 37 minutes 30 seconds behind
54. Arnaud	(VC)	1h 37 minutes 50 seconds behind
55. Menthéour	(Ren)	1h 38 minutes 51 seconds behind
56. Kuiper	(Kwa)	1h 39 minutes 30 seconds behind
57. Peeters	(Kwa)	1h 39 minutes 59 seconds behind
58. Zimmerman	(Cil)	1h 40 minutes 39 seconds behind
59. De Rooy	(Pan)	1h 42 minutes 20 seconds behind
60. Loayza	(Col)	1h 43 minutes 55 seconds behind
61. Ferreti	(Cil)	1h 47 minutes 24 seconds behind
62. Le Guilloux	(VC)	1h 48 minutes 38 seconds behind
63. Gallopin	(Ski)	1h 49 minutes 7 seconds behind
64. Dietzen	(Tek)	1h 49 minutes 31 seconds behind
65. Lopez	(Col)	1h 49 minutes 59 seconds behind
66. Coll	(Tek)	1h 52 minutes 4 seconds behind
67. Chappuis	(Sys)	1h 52 minutes 4 seconds behind
68. Martens	(Tek)	1h 52 minutes 25 seconds behind
69. Frébert	(Sys)	1h 53 minutes 58 seconds behind
70. Santoni	(Car)	1h 54 minutes 26 seconds behind
71. Hernandez-Ubeda	(Rey)	1h 55 minutes 17 seconds behind
72. Didier	(Ren)	1h 56 minutes 39 seconds behind

73. Vallet	(VC)	1h 58 minutes 23 seconds behind
74. De Wolf	(Eur)	1h 58 minutes 36 seconds behind
75. Van Vliet	(Kwa)	1h 58 minutes 52 seconds behind
76. Leali	(Car)	2h 3 minutes 40 seconds behind
77. Chagas	(Spo)	2h 8 minutes 13 seconds behind
78. Corredor	(Col)	2h 9 minutes 31 seconds behind
79. Clerc	(Ski)	2h 11 minutes 29 seconds behind
80. Poisson	(Ren)	2h 11 minutes 37 seconds behind
81. Perini	(Car)	2h 12 minutes 8 seconds behind
82. Rault	(VC)	2h 12 minutes 17 seconds behind
83. Dithurbide	(Spo)	2h 13 minutes 2 seconds behind
84. Maechler	(Cil)	2h 15 minutes 23 seconds behind
85. Bonnet	(Sys)	2h 17 minutes 18 seconds behind
86. Bourreau	(Peu)	2h 20 minutes 29 seconds behind
87. Greciano	(Rey)	2h 20 minutes 51 seconds behind
88. Devos	(Spl)	2h 23 minutes 55 seconds behind
89. Brun	(Peu)	2h 25 minutes 8 seconds behind
90. Vanderaerden	(Pan)	2h 26 minutes 14 seconds behind
91. Yates	(Peu)	2h 26 minutes 41 seconds behind
92. De Keulenaar	(Pan)	2h 28 minutes 49 seconds behind
93. Lang	(Car)	2h 29 minutes 21 seconds behind
94. Zeferino	(Spo)	2h 29 minutes 26 seconds behind
95. Peiper	(Peu)	2h 31 minutes 28 seconds behind
96. Moerlen	(Ski)	2h 31 minutes 33 seconds behind
97. Gauthier	(Cop)	2h 34 minutes 10 seconds behind
98. Alfonsel	(Tek)	2h 35 minutes 25 seconds behind
99. Bondue	(Red)	2h 36 minutes 45 seconds behind
100. Hoste	(Eur)	2h 38 minutes 8 seconds behind
101. Hanegraaf	(Kwa)	2h 44 minutes 4 seconds behind
102. Bossis	(Peu)	2h 44 minutes 26 seconds behind
103. Knetemann	(Eur)	2h 47 minutes 58 seconds behind
104. Dierickx	(Eur)	2h 49 minutes 20 seconds behind
105. Castaing	(Peu)	2h 51 minutes 59 seconds behind
106. Van den Haute	(Red)	2h 52 minutes 48 seconds behind
107. Manders	(Kwa)	2h 59 minutes 1 seconds behind
108. Wijnands	(Kwa)	3h 1 minute 4 seconds behind
109. Govaerts	(Eur)	3h 1 minute 39 seconds behind
110. Levavasseur	(Red)	3h 3 minutes 4 seconds behind

111.	Régis Simon	(Red)	3h 4 minutes 25 seconds behind
112.	Linard	(Peu)	3h 6 minutes 24 seconds behind
113.	Lualdi	(Car)	3h 6 minutes 50 seconds behind
114.	Moreau	(Cop)	3h 7 minutes 34 seconds behind
115.	Thévenard	(Spo)	3h 9 minutes 16 seconds behind
116.	Sherwen	(Red)	3h 24 minutes 48 seconds behind
117.	Charréard	(Spo)	3h 25 minutes 18 seconds behind
118.	Correla	(Spo)	3h 25 minutes 37 seconds behind
119.	Xavier	(Spo)	3h 27 minutes 26 seconds behind
120.	Urrutibeazcoa	(Tek)	3h 30 minutes 11 seconds behind
121.	Gaigne	(Ren)	3h 35 minutes 39 seconds behind
122.	Marta	(Spo)	3h 40 minutes 5 seconds behind
123.	Russenberger	(Cil)	4h 0 minutes 30 seconds behind
124.	Glaus	(Cil)	4h 1 minute 17 seconds behind

Team abbreviations: Ren = Renault, VC = La Vie Claire,
Peu = Peugeot, Ski = Skil, Rey = Reynolds, Tek = Teka,
Spl = Splendor, Spo = Sporting Lisbon, Col = Colombia, Cop = Coop,
Cil = Cilo-Aufina, Car = Carrera-Inoxpran, Pan = Panasonic,
Kwa = Kwantum, Sys = Système U, Red = La Redoute,
Eur = Europ Décor.

FINAL OVERALL STANDINGS FOR LEADING CLIMBERS
(POLKA-DOT JERSEY)

1.	Millar	(Peu)	284 points
2.	Fignon	(Ren)	212 points
3.	Arroyo	(Rey)	140 points
4.	Herrera	(Col)	108 points
5.	Jiminez	(Tek)	92 points
6.	Hinault	(VC)	89 points
7.	Pascal Simon	(Peu)	79 points
8.	De Rooy	(Pan)	74 points
9.	LeMond	(Ren)	68 points
10.	Kelly	(Ski)	65 points

FINAL OVERALL STANDINGS FOR POINTS LEADERS

(GREEN JERSEY)

1.	Hoste	(Eur)	322 points
2.	Kelly	(Ski)	318 points
3.	Vanderaerden	(Pan)	247 points
4.	Van Vliet	(Kwa)	173 points
5.	Hinault	(VC)	146 points
6.	Fignon	(Ren)	143 points
7.	Castaing	(Peu)	137 points
8.	Jules	(Ren)	123 points
9.	Rault	(VC)	83 points
10.	Van Den Brande	(Spl)	80 points

FINAL OVERALL STANDINGS FOR LEADING NEOPHYTES

(WHITE JERSEY)

1. LeMond   (Ren)

2. Munoz   (Tek)

3. Ruttimann (VC)

FINAL OVERALL STANDINGS OF TEAMS BY POINTS

1. Panasonic-Raleigh
2. Renault
3. Peugeot
4. Skil
5. La Vie Claire
6. Kwantum
7. Reynolds
8. Splendor

9. Coop
10. Teka
11. La Redoute
12. Système U
13. Europ Decor
14. Carrera-Inoxpran
15. Cilo-Aufina
16. Colombia
17. Sporting Lisbon

FINAL OVERALL STANDINGS OF TEAMS BY OVERALL TIME

1. Renault
2. Skil
3. Reynolds
4. Peugeot
5. La Vie Claire
6. Panasonic-Raleigh
7. Colombia
8. Teka
9. Splendor
10. Cilo-Aufina
11. Coop
12. La Redoute
13. Système U
14. Kwantum
15. Carrera-Inoxpran
16. Europ Decor
17. Sporting Lisbon

About the Author

SAMUEL ABT, a deputy editor of the *International Herald Tribune* in Paris, has written about the Tour de France for that newspaper and for the *New York Times* since 1977. Before he moved to France in 1971 he was a copyeditor for several newspapers in New England, for the *Baltimore Sun* and for the *New York Times.* A graduate of Brown University, he has also been a Professional Journalism Fellow at Stanford University.